History of American Football & the NFL Step by Step

A Chronological Evolution of America's Game

Ken Patton

PREFACE

Welcome, football fans and curious readers! You're about to go on an exciting trip through the history of America's favorite game. Whether you're a die-hard fan who can recite stats in your sleep or someone who's just starting to learn about the sport, this book is for you.

"History of American Football & the NFL Step by Step: A Chronological Evolution of America's Game" is exactly what it sounds like – a walk through time, exploring how a simple game grew into the massive cultural phenomenon we know today. We're going to start way back before the NFL even existed and travel all the way to the present day, looking at all the twists and turns along the way.

Now, you might be thinking, "History? Isn't that boring?" Not when it comes to football! This isn't just a dry collection of dates and names. It's a story filled with larger-than-life characters, intense rivalries, game-changing innovations, and moments that had millions of fans holding their breath. We'll look at how the rules of the game evolved, how strategies changed over time, and how football became intertwined with American culture.

In these pages, you'll meet the pioneers who shaped the game in its early days, like Walter Camp, often called the "Father of American Football." You'll relive the excitement of the first Super Bowl and see how it grew into the massive event it is today. We'll explore how television changed the way we watch football and how fantasy leagues have given fans a new way to engage with the sport.

But it's not all touchdowns and glory. We'll also tackle some of the challenges the sport has faced. We'll look at how the NFL has dealt with issues like player safety, social activism, and financial disputes. By understanding these challenges, you'll get a fuller picture of the complexity of professional football.

One of the things that makes football so fascinating is how it's constantly evolving. New strategies, new technologies, new rules – the game today looks very different from how it did even 20 years ago, let alone when it first started. We'll trace these changes step by step, helping you understand not just what changed, but why.

As we move through the decades, you'll see how football has reflected and sometimes shaped American society. From its role during wartime to its place in Thanksgiving traditions, from civil rights movements to modern-day activism, football has been there through it all.

By the time you finish this book, you'll have a deeper appreciation for the game you love (or are starting to love). You'll understand the context behind today's NFL and have some great stories to share at your next tailgate party or family gathering.

We've also designed the book to be read non-continuously, if desired, where each chapter and even each section can stand on its own. You might see some mild repetition here and there within chapters to help support this reading style. So feel free to skip around if you wish.

So, grab your favorite snacks (because what's football without snacks?), get comfortable, and let's kick off this journey through the history of American football. Whether you're reading this to boost your football knowledge, to understand why your partner or friends are so obsessed with the game, or just out of curiosity, I hope you'll find it as exciting and engaging as the game itself.

TOPICAL OUTLINE

Chapter 1: Origins and Early Development (Pre-1900)
- The Roots in Rugby and Soccer
- The First College Football Game
- The Role of Ivy League Schools
- Walter Camp: The Father of American Football
- Early Rule Changes and Innovations
- The Formation of the Intercollegiate Football Association (IFA)
- Early Safety Concerns and the Need for Reform
- The Rise of Regional Football Rivalries
- The Popularization of Football in Colleges
- The Emergence of Professional Football

Chapter 2: The Birth of Professional Football (1900-1920)
- The First Professional Teams
- The Formation of the Ohio League
- The Establishment of the American Professional Football Association (APFA)
- Key Early Players and Influencers
- Challenges of Legitimacy and Recognition
- The Role of Early Stadiums and Infrastructure

Chapter 3: The NFL is Born (1920s)
- Transition from APFA to NFL
- Early NFL Teams and Founding Members
- The Role of George Halas
- The NFL's Struggles in the Early Years
- Popularity Compared to Baseball
- The Red Grange Impact

Chapter 4: The 1930s - Survival and Growth
- The NFL's Financial Struggles During the Great Depression
- Introduction of the NFL Draft
- The Birth of the Chicago Bears Dynasty
- The First NFL Championship Game
- Innovations in the Passing Game
- The Introduction of the Forward Pass

Chapter 5: World War II and the NFL (1940s)
- The Impact of the War on the NFL
- The NFL's Wartime Teams and Roster Challenges

- Post-War NFL Expansion
- The Birth of the Cleveland Browns
- The 1946 Championship Game

Chapter 6: The 1950s - A Decade of Change

- The NFL-AFL Rivalry Begins
- The Rise of Television and Football
- The Legendary 1958 NFL Championship Game
- The Growth of NFL Popularity
- Key Players and Teams of the 1950s
- The Rise of the Two-Platoon System
- Strategic & Schematic Evolutions in the 1950s

Chapter 7: The AFL and NFL Merger (1960s)

- The Formation of the AFL
- Early AFL-NFL Competition
- Key Figures in the Merger
- The Super Bowl is Born
- The Significance of the Merger for American Football
- Strategic & Schematic Evolutions in the 1960s

Chapter 8: The Super Bowl Era Begins (1970s)

- The Emergence of the Super Bowl as a National Event
- Dominant Teams of the 1970s
- Key Players of the Decade
- NFL Rule Changes and Their Impact
- The Rise of Monday Night Football
- The Impact of the NFL Players Association
- Strategic & Schematic Evolutions in the 1970s

Chapter 9: The 1980s - Expansion and Scandal

- The NFL Expands to New Markets
- The Influence of the West Coast Offense & 49ers Dominance
- The USFL Challenge and Collapse
- The NFL Players Strike of 1982
- Strategic & Schematic Evolutions in the 1980s

Chapter 10: The 1990s - The Globalization of the NFL

- Expansion Teams and Market Growth
- The Rise of the Dallas Cowboys Dynasty
- The Impact of Free Agency on the NFL
- International Games and NFL Europe
- The 1994 Salary Cap Introduction
- The Introduction of Instant Replay

- Strategic & Schematic Evolutions in the 1990s

Chapter 11: The 2000s - The Era of Parity

- The Rise of the New England Patriots Dynasty
- The Impact of Technology on the Game
- The Growth of Fantasy Football
- The Changing Landscape of NFL Broadcasting
- Strategic & Schematic Evolutions in the 2000s

Chapter 12: The 2010s - Social Issues and the NFL

- The NFL's Response to Concussions and CTE
- The Rise of Player Activism
- The Expansion of the Regular Season
- Strategic & Schematic Evolutions in the 2010s

Chapter 13: The Modern NFL (2020-Present)

- The Impact of the COVID-19 Pandemic
- The NFL's Embrace of Technology and Data Analytics
- Ongoing Rule Changes and Safety Measures
- The Global Expansion Strategy
- The Future of the NFL
- Strategic & Schematic Evolutions in the 2020s

Chapter 14: The NFL's Cultural Influence

- The NFL's Role in American Pop Culture
- The Influence of NFL Films and Media
- Football as a Thanksgiving Tradition
- The Super Bowl Halftime Show and Advertisements
- The NFL's Impact on Youth and College Football

Chapter 15: The Economics of the NFL

- The Business of NFL Broadcasting Rights
- The NFL's Revenue Sharing Model
- The Economic Impact of Hosting an NFL Team
- The Financial Dynamics of the Super Bowl
- Sponsorship and Endorsement Deals

Chapter 16: The Legacy and Future of American Football

- The Hall of Fame and Honoring NFL Legends
- The Ongoing Debate Over Player Safety
- The NFL's Role in Promoting Diversity and Inclusion
- The Evolution of NFL Coaching and Strategy
- The Future of American Football: Challenges and Opportunities

Chapter 17: American Football Timelines

- Timeline of Major Events in Football's Evolution
- Timeline of Strategic Evolutions in Football

Afterword

TABLE OF CONTENTS

Chapter 1: Origins and Early Development (Pre-1900) ... 1
Chapter 2: The Birth of Professional Football (1900-1920) ... 15
Chapter 3: The NFL is Born (1920s) ... 24
Chapter 4: The 1930s - Survival and Growth ... 31
Chapter 5: World War II and the NFL (1940s) ... 38
Chapter 6: The 1950s - A Decade of Change ... 44
Chapter 7: The AFL and NFL Merger (1960s) ... 53
Chapter 8: The Super Bowl Era Begins (1970s) ... 61
Chapter 9: The 1980s - Expansion and Scandal ... 69
Chapter 10: The 1990s - The Globalization of the NFL ... 75
Chapter 11: The 2000s - The Era of Parity ... 82
Chapter 12: The 2010s - Social Issues and the NFL ... 87
Chapter 13: The Modern NFL (2020-Present) ... 91
Chapter 14: The NFL's Cultural Influence ... 97
Chapter 15: The Economics of the NFL ... 102
Chapter 16: The Legacy and Future of American Football ... 107
Chapter 17: American Football Timelines ... 112
Afterword ... 122

CHAPTER 1: ORIGINS AND EARLY DEVELOPMENT (PRE-1900)

The Roots in Rugby and Soccer

The origins of American football trace back to the 19th century, deeply intertwined with the sports of rugby and soccer. These sports, born on the fields of English public schools, were not just pastimes but rituals that shaped young men into disciplined, strong individuals. They were rough, chaotic, and often played with little regard for what we would now call "rules." Over time, however, these games evolved, becoming more structured and ultimately giving rise to the distinct sport of American football.

Soccer, or association football, was the first to gain prominence. By the early 1800s, it had become a widely accepted game in British schools. The objective was simple: two teams tried to kick a ball into the opposing team's goal. The game was more about skill and teamwork than physical dominance. The rules, formalized in 1863 by the newly founded Football Association (FA) in England, emphasized this by banning the use of hands and limiting physical contact. Soccer's popularity spread quickly, and by the mid-19th century, it had crossed the Atlantic to the United States.

In the U.S., soccer was initially embraced by colleges and universities. But American institutions were also experimenting with another game: **rugby**. Unlike soccer, rugby allowed players to carry the ball and emphasized physical strength and endurance. It was a game of scrums, tackles, and mauls—violent by nature and demanding toughness. The Rugby Football Union (RFU) was established in England in 1871 to codify its rules, but by then, the game had already gained a foothold in America, where it would eventually merge with elements of soccer to form the early version of American football.

The first recorded game of what would become American football took place on November 6, 1869, between Rutgers and Princeton. This game resembled soccer more than rugby, with players mainly kicking the ball and trying to score by getting it into the opponent's goal. However, the game's rules varied widely between colleges, and there was little consistency from one match to another. This lack of standardization created the perfect environment for experimentation and the blending of soccer and rugby elements.

As the 1870s progressed, **Harvard University** had an important part in this evolution. Harvard preferred a version of rugby that allowed carrying the ball, and when they played against Canada's McGill University in 1874, the match featured both kicking and carrying the ball. This hybrid style, which blended the kicking of soccer with the physicality of rugby, appealed to American players and began to gain popularity.

Walter Camp, often called the "Father of American Football," entered the scene during this period. A Yale student and athlete, Camp was instrumental in shaping the rules of the game. In the late 1870s and early 1880s, he advocated for several key changes that would distinguish American football from its English counterparts. One of Camp's most significant contributions was the introduction of the line of scrimmage, which established a clear point of contest between the two teams. This innovation, borrowed conceptually from rugby's scrums, gave American football a distinct strategic complexity. Camp also introduced the idea of downs and the requirement to advance the ball a certain distance within a set number of plays, further setting the sport apart.

By the 1880s, American football had clearly diverged from both rugby and soccer. The game now involved more organized plays, the forward pass was still decades away, but teams were beginning to specialize in certain styles of play. Rugby's influence remained, particularly in the emphasis on physical contact, but American football had taken on its own identity.

Throughout the 19th century, American football continued to evolve, often in response to the high level of violence associated with rugby-style play. Rules were continuously refined to make the game safer and more structured. By the end of the 1800s, what had started as a mix of rugby and soccer had transformed into a distinct sport, with its unique rules, strategies, and culture.

The roots of American football are deeply embedded in rugby and soccer, but the sport's rapid evolution during the late 19th century ensured it would develop its own identity. The changes implemented during this period laid the foundation for the modern game, setting the stage for American football to become one of the most popular sports in the United States.

The First College Football Game

On November 6, 1869, a crowd gathered in New Brunswick, New Jersey, to witness what would go down in history as the first-ever college football game. The match took place between Rutgers College and the College of New Jersey, now known as Princeton University. But this was not football as we know it today. As mentioned, the game played on that chilly afternoon was more akin to soccer than the gridiron spectacle that would evolve in the decades to come.

The match was organized under a set of rules borrowed from the London Football Association, the governing body for soccer in England. There were 25 players on each team, a far cry from the 11-a-side game familiar to modern football fans. The objective was simple: kick the ball into the opponent's goal. There was no carrying the ball, no blocking, and no line of scrimmage. Players could not pass the ball with their hands, and the only way to advance was to kick it forward. It was a game of endurance, with teams scrapping for control of the ball, using their feet and bodies in a chaotic scramble to score.

The rules were set up by the Rutgers students who hosted the match. They chose to use a round soccer ball rather than an oval one, which would later become the norm in American football. The game was played on a roughly 120-yard field, divided by a midpoint line. The first team to score six goals would be declared the winner.

The match began with Rutgers kicking off to Princeton. As soon as the ball was in play, it became clear that this was not a gentlemanly game of soccer. The players quickly adopted a more aggressive style, shoving and pushing to gain control of the ball. Rutgers scored the first goal, much to the delight of the home crowd. Princeton answered with a goal of their own, and the game was on. The teams traded goals in a back-and-forth battle, with Rutgers ultimately emerging victorious, winning by a score of 6-4.

This first game was a momentous event, but it was not an immediate sensation. The rules of the game varied significantly from one college to another, and there was no standardized version of the sport. In fact, after the game, Princeton and Rutgers did not play each other again for several years. The match was largely forgotten in the immediate aftermath, with other colleges continuing to play their own versions of football, which often bore little resemblance to the game played in New Brunswick.

However, this match planted the seed for what would eventually become American football. Over the next few years, other colleges began to take an interest in the sport. As more schools participated, the need for standardized rules became apparent. Meetings were held to discuss and codify the rules, leading to the creation of the Intercollegiate Football Association (IFA) in 1876, where many of the fundamental principles of the game, such as the line of scrimmage and the concept of downs, were first introduced.

While the first college football game in 1869 was a modest affair, it marked the beginning of a journey that would see American football evolve into one of the most popular and iconic sports in the United States. The chaotic, rough-and-tumble game played that day in New Brunswick bore little resemblance to the highly organized and strategic sport it would become, but it was the spark that ignited a new sporting tradition.

The Role of Ivy League Schools

The Ivy League schools had an important part in the early development and formalization of American football. In the late 19th century, these prestigious institutions were not just centers of academic excellence but also the birthplace of many of the traditions and innovations that shaped the sport. Their influence extended beyond their own campuses, setting standards that would be adopted by colleges and universities across the country.

In the years following the first college football game in 1869, the Ivy League schools—Harvard, Yale, Princeton, and others—began to take a keen interest in the sport. However, each school played by its own set of rules, leading to significant variations in how the game was played. Harvard, for example, favored a version that closely resembled rugby, allowing players to carry the ball, while other schools, like Princeton, played a game that was more similar to soccer. These differences made it difficult for schools to compete against each other, as they often had to agree on which set of rules to use before each match.

The turning point came in 1874 when Harvard played a series of games against McGill University from Canada. McGill played by rugby rules, which Harvard found appealing due to the physicality and strategic depth of the game. After these matches, Harvard adopted rugby-style rules for their games, setting a new standard for the sport. This decision by Harvard marked a significant shift in the development of American football, moving it away from soccer and closer to the game we recognize today.

Yale, under the leadership of Walter Camp, quickly followed suit. Camp, who would later be known as the "Father of American Football," was instrumental in formalizing the rules of the game. In 1876, representatives from Harvard, Yale, Princeton, and Columbia met in Springfield, Massachusetts, to form the Intercollegiate Football Association (IFA). This organization aimed to standardize the rules of the game across colleges. The IFA adopted a set of rules that were heavily influenced by rugby but also included innovations such as the line of scrimmage, which Camp proposed. The introduction of the line of scrimmage was a key moment, as it defined the offensive and defensive sides and introduced a new level of strategy to the game.

The Ivy League schools did more than just shape the rules of football; they also popularized the sport. The intense rivalries between these schools, particularly the annual Harvard-Yale game, captured the public's imagination. These games drew large crowds and received significant coverage in newspapers, helping to spread the sport's popularity beyond the Northeast. The prestige of the Ivy League also played a role in legitimizing football as a serious sport, worthy of attention and respect.

As football continued to evolve, the Ivy League schools remained at the forefront of innovation. They were among the first to establish formal athletic programs, build dedicated football stadiums, and hire professional coaches. These developments helped to institutionalize football as a key part of college life, not just in the Ivy League but across the country.

In the early 20th century, concerns about the safety of football led to calls for reform. Once again, the Ivy League schools were at the center of this movement. Harvard's president, Charles Eliot, was a vocal critic of the sport's brutality, and his concerns, along with those of other Ivy League administrators, led to the formation of the NCAA in 1906. The NCAA introduced new rules to reduce violence in the game, such as the legalization of the forward pass, which made the game safer and more dynamic.

The Ivy League's role in the development of American football cannot be overstated. From the early adoption of rugby rules to the formalization of the sport through the IFA and the creation of the NCAA, these schools were instrumental in shaping the game. Their influence ensured that football would not only survive but thrive, becoming a central part of American culture and identity.

Walter Camp: The Father of American Football

Walter Camp is widely recognized as the "Father of American Football," a title earned through his profound influence on the development of the sport. Born in New Haven, Connecticut, in 1859, Camp's early exposure to sports at Yale University laid the foundation for his future contributions to football. His time as a player, coach, and administrator provided him with a unique perspective that allowed him to shape the game in ways that continue to resonate today.

Camp's journey with football began when he enrolled at Yale in 1876. At the time, the game was still evolving from its roots in rugby and soccer, with no standardized rules. Camp, who played as a halfback, quickly distinguished himself not only on the field but also in the administrative side of the sport. His strategic mind and passion for the game led him to become the team captain, a position equivalent to the modern-day head coach. This role gave him the authority to influence the way the game was played, and Camp wasted no time in making his mark.

As mentioned, one of Camp's most significant contributions was his role in the establishment of the Intercollegiate Football Association (IFA) in 1876, alongside representatives from Harvard, Princeton, and Columbia. The IFA aimed to standardize the rules of the game, which varied significantly between colleges. Camp's input was crucial in these discussions, and he pushed for rules that would make the game more organized and strategic. His ideas were often influenced by his desire to create a sport that combined the physicality of rugby with the tactical depth of a more structured game.

Camp's most enduring legacy is the introduction of the line of scrimmage. Before this innovation, football games often devolved into chaotic scrums, with no clear separation between the offensive and defensive sides. Camp proposed the line of scrimmage to create a more orderly and predictable game, where each team would have a fair chance to advance the ball. This change also introduced a new level of strategy, as teams had to carefully plan their plays, knowing that they had a set number of downs to gain ten yards and retain possession.

Camp didn't stop there. He also introduced the concept of downs and the requirement to gain a specific distance within a set number of plays. Initially, teams had three downs to gain five yards. This rule, which would later evolve into the modern four downs to gain ten yards, forced teams to think tactically about each play, rather than relying solely on brute force to move the ball. This shift transformed football from a brawl into a game of strategy, where careful planning and execution became just as important as physical strength.

Another of Camp's innovations was the creation of the quarterback position. In the early versions of the game, all players had relatively equal roles in advancing the ball. Camp recognized the need for a leader on the field, someone who could make quick decisions and direct the team's plays. The quarterback became that leader, responsible for calling the plays and executing the strategies devised by the coach. This role not only added a new layer of strategy to the game but also helped to humanize it, as fans could now identify with a central figure who embodied the team's fortunes.

Camp's influence extended beyond the rules of the game. He was also instrumental in popularizing football through his writing and advocacy. He authored numerous books and articles on football, sharing his knowledge and passion for the game with a broader audience. His writings helped to standardize the sport across the country, ensuring that the same game was being played from coast to coast.

Moreover, Camp's contributions weren't limited to the early years of football. He continued to be involved in the sport throughout his life, serving on rules committees and remaining an influential figure in the development of the game until his death in 1925. His work laid the foundation for the modern game of football, transforming it from a chaotic, disorganized contest into a highly strategic and regulated sport. The innovations he introduced—such as the line of scrimmage, the system of downs, and the quarterback position—are still central to the game today.

Early Rule Changes and Innovations

The forward pass, while not fully legalized until the early 20th century, also began to take shape during this period. Initially, football was a game dominated by running plays, with teams relying on brute force to advance the ball. However, as the game evolved, the idea of passing the ball forward began to gain traction as a way to outmaneuver defenses. The forward pass added a new dimension to the game, allowing teams to stretch the field vertically and introduce a level of unpredictability that had previously been absent. Though its use was limited in the early years, the forward pass would eventually become a cornerstone of the sport, revolutionizing offensive play and opening up new strategic possibilities.

The early years of football also saw the introduction of more formalized rules governing player safety and conduct. As the sport grew in popularity, concerns about its violence and the number of injuries led to calls for reform. Rules were implemented to limit dangerous plays, such as the flying wedge, a formation that often led to serious injuries. The establishment of these rules helped to make the game safer and more sustainable in the long term, ensuring that it could continue to grow and evolve without being banned or excessively regulated.

These early rule changes and innovations were crucial in transforming football from a chaotic and often dangerous contest into a highly strategic and regulated sport. Each innovation added a new layer of complexity and structure to the game, making it more enjoyable for players and spectators alike. The foundation laid by these changes allowed football to grow into the dominant sport it is today, with a rich history of strategic depth and innovation that continues to evolve with each passing season.

The Formation of the Intercollegiate Football Association (IFA)

The formation of the Intercollegiate Football Association (IFA) in 1876 marked a critical moment in the development of American football. Before its establishment, college football was a disorganized and chaotic sport, with each school playing by its own set of rules. This lack of uniformity made it difficult for colleges to compete against each other, as they often had to agree on which rules to use before each match. The IFA was created to address this problem by standardizing the rules across participating colleges, paving the way for the modern game of football.

The IFA was born out of a meeting held in Springfield, Massachusetts, on November 23, 1876. Representatives from four colleges—Harvard, Yale, Princeton, and Columbia—gathered to discuss the future of the sport. These schools were among the most prominent in the country, and their involvement lent significant credibility to the organization. The meeting was largely influenced by the success of the Rugby Football Union (RFU) in England, which had been formed in 1871 to standardize the rules of rugby. The founders of the IFA sought to create a similar body for American football, one that would bring order to the game and facilitate intercollegiate competition.

At the meeting, the representatives agreed to adopt a modified version of the rules used by the RFU. This decision was heavily influenced by Harvard, which had played a series of games against McGill University from Canada in 1874. The McGill team played by rugby rules, and Harvard found this style of play appealing. The adoption of these rules by the IFA signaled a move away from the soccer-like games that had been popular in the early days of American football, bringing the sport closer to the version we recognize today.

One of the key innovations introduced by the IFA was the concept of the line of scrimmage, an idea championed by Walter Camp, who was a student at Yale at the time. The line of scrimmage created a clear division between the offensive and defensive teams, providing a structured starting point for each play. This rule was a significant departure from rugby, where play often began with a chaotic scrum. The line of scrimmage introduced a new level of strategy to the game, as teams now had to plan their plays with a defined point of attack.

Another important rule adopted by the IFA was the system of downs. Under this system, a team had three downs to advance the ball five yards. If they succeeded, they were awarded a new set of downs; if they failed, the other team took possession of the ball. This rule was a major innovation, as it required teams to think strategically about each play, rather than relying solely on brute force to advance the ball. The system of downs added a layer of complexity to the game, making it more engaging for both players and spectators.

The formation of the IFA was a turning point in the history of American football. It provided the sport with a formal structure and set of rules, allowing it to grow and develop in a more organized manner. The standardized rules facilitated intercollegiate competition, leading to the establishment of longstanding rivalries and the growth of football as a major college sport. The IFA's influence extended far beyond its founding members, as other colleges across the country began to adopt its rules, helping to spread the sport nationwide.

While the IFA was eventually dissolved in the early 20th century as the sport continued to evolve, its legacy lives on. The rules and structures it introduced laid the foundation for the modern game of football, and its role in the sport's early development cannot be overstated. The formation of the IFA was a crucial step in transforming football from a disorganized pastime into the highly strategic and popular sport it is today.

Early Safety Concerns and the Need for Reform

The early years of American football were marked by intense physicality and violence, leading to widespread concerns about player safety. The sport was inherently rough, with players often sustaining serious injuries during games. By the late 19th century, the rising number of injuries and even fatalities on the field sparked a national debate about the need for reform in football, ultimately leading to significant changes in the way the game was played.

Football in the late 1800s was a brutal sport. The lack of protective equipment and the emphasis on physical dominance meant that injuries were common. Players suffered broken bones, concussions, and other serious injuries on a regular basis. The style of play was often reckless, with teams using formations like the "flying wedge," where players would form a V-shaped wall to plow through the opposing team. This tactic was highly effective but extremely dangerous, leading to numerous injuries.

The growing concern over the safety of football reached a tipping point in 1905. That year, 19 players died from injuries sustained during games, and many more were seriously injured. The public outcry was intense, with newspapers across the country calling for the sport to be banned. Prominent figures, including President Theodore Roosevelt, who was an ardent supporter of the sport, recognized that changes were necessary to save football from extinction. Roosevelt, a known advocate for physical fitness and competitive sports, convened a meeting with representatives from Harvard, Yale, and Princeton to discuss how to make the game safer.

The outcome of this meeting, along with other similar gatherings, was the formation of the Intercollegiate Athletic Association of the United States (IAAUS) in 1906, which would later become the National Collegiate Athletic Association (NCAA). The IAAUS was tasked with overseeing college sports and implementing reforms to reduce the violence in football. Before the forward pass, football was primarily a running game, with teams relying on mass formations and brute force to advance the ball. The forward pass introduced a new, less dangerous way to move the ball downfield, reducing the reliance on physical collisions.

In addition to the forward pass, several other rule changes were implemented to improve player safety. The neutral zone was introduced, creating space between the offensive and defensive lines at the start of each play, reducing the likelihood of violent collisions. The number of players on the field was also reduced from 15 to 11, further decreasing the density of players and the potential for injury. The flying wedge and other dangerous formations were banned, as they were deemed too risky.

These reforms had a profound impact on the game. The introduction of the forward pass not only made football safer but also transformed it into a more dynamic and strategic sport. Teams could now use a variety of plays to move the ball, adding a new level of excitement to the game. The reduction in injuries helped to quell the calls for football to be banned, allowing the sport to continue growing in popularity.

However, the safety concerns were far from fully addressed. Football remained a physically demanding and dangerous sport, and discussions about player safety continued throughout the 20th century and into the present day. The reforms of the early 1900s laid the groundwork for ongoing efforts to protect players while preserving the integrity of the game. The early safety concerns and the subsequent reforms were pivotal in shaping the direction of American football, ensuring that it could evolve into a safer, more sustainable sport while maintaining its competitive spirit and appeal.

The Rise of Regional Football Rivalries

In the late 19th and early 20th centuries, regional football rivalries began to emerge as a defining feature of American college football. These rivalries, often rooted in geographic proximity and long-standing institutional competition, were important in popularizing the sport and deepening its cultural significance. The intensity and passion surrounding these games captured the public's imagination, transforming football from a mere pastime into a central part of American collegiate life.

One of the earliest and most famous of these rivalries was the annual contest between Harvard and Yale, known simply as "The Game." This rivalry began in 1875, just a few years after the sport had started to gain traction in American colleges. Harvard and Yale, two of the most prestigious institutions in the country, were natural competitors both on and off the field. Their football games quickly became more than just sporting events; they were social occasions that drew large crowds and garnered significant media attention. The fierce competition between these two schools set the stage for the development of similar rivalries across the country.

As football spread to other regions, so did the concept of regional rivalries. The Midwest saw the rise of the Michigan-Ohio State rivalry, which began in 1897. This rivalry, now known as "The Game" in the Midwest, grew out of a broader cultural and economic competition between the two states. The intensity of the games, combined with the passionate fan bases of both schools, made this rivalry one of the most significant in college football history. The annual matchup became a focal point of the season for both teams, often determining conference championships and influencing national rankings.

In the South, the Alabama-Auburn rivalry, known as the "Iron Bowl," began in 1893. This rivalry reflected the deep-seated pride and competitive spirit of the region, where football was quickly becoming a cultural phenomenon. The Iron Bowl, like other regional rivalries, was more than just a game; it was an event that brought entire communities together, sometimes dividing families and friends for a day. The importance of these games in the lives of fans cannot be overstated, as they often represented much more than athletic competition—they were a source of identity and pride.

These regional rivalries were not limited to just the most famous matchups. Across the country, schools began to develop their own local rivalries, each with its own unique history and traditions. The Army-Navy game, first played in 1890, became another iconic rivalry, symbolizing the friendly yet intense competition between the U.S. Military Academy and the U.S. Naval Academy. These games, steeped in tradition and pageantry, became must-watch events that attracted national attention.

The rise of regional rivalries also had a significant impact on the growth of college football. These games generated immense interest and excitement, drawing large crowds and increasing the visibility of the sport. Rivalry games were often the highlight of the season, with newspapers dedicating extensive coverage to the buildup and aftermath of the contests. The passion surrounding these games helped to solidify football's place in American culture, ensuring its continued growth and popularity.

Moreover, the rivalries fostered a sense of community and belonging among fans, who saw their support for their team as an expression of regional pride. The intense emotions associated with these games made them more than just sporting events—they were cultural touchstones that brought people together, creating a shared experience that transcended the outcome of the game.

The emergence of regional football rivalries played a vital role in shaping the early history of American college football. These rivalries not only fueled the sport's growth but also embedded it deeply into the fabric of American culture. The traditions and passions born out of these early rivalries continue to influence the sport today, making them an enduring legacy of college football's formative years.

The Popularization of Football in Colleges

The popularization of football in American colleges during the late 19th and early 20th centuries was a transformative period that established the sport as a cornerstone of collegiate life. This rise in popularity was driven by a combination of factors, including the formation of organized leagues, the growing appeal of intercollegiate competition, and the intense rivalries that captured the public's imagination.

Initially, the sport was seen as a way to foster physical fitness and camaraderie among students. However, as the game evolved, it began to attract more attention and enthusiasm from both players and spectators.

As football spread to more colleges across the country, the intercollegiate competition became a significant aspect of college life. Games were often major social events, drawing large crowds of students, alumni, and local community members. The excitement surrounding these games was amplified by the formation of regional rivalries, such as the Harvard-Yale and Michigan-Ohio State matchups. These rivalries became defining aspects of the college football experience, with games often deciding conference championships and earning national attention.

The popularity of football in colleges was also bolstered by the role it played in the broader cultural and social life of the institutions. Football games became key events on college campuses, often tied to homecoming celebrations and other significant milestones in the academic calendar. The games provided a platform for school spirit and unity, as students and alumni rallied behind their teams. This sense of community and shared identity was a powerful force that helped to embed football deeply into the fabric of college life.

Moreover, the rise of college football was closely linked to the development of athletic programs and facilities. As the sport grew in popularity, colleges began to invest more resources into their football teams, building dedicated stadiums and hiring professional coaches. This investment not only improved the quality of play but also enhanced the spectacle of the games, attracting even larger crowds and further boosting the sport's popularity. The construction of iconic stadiums, such as the Yale Bowl in 1914 and Michigan Stadium in 1927, symbolized the central place that football had come to occupy in college life.

The media also had a significant part in the popularization of college football. Newspapers began to cover the sport extensively, dedicating entire sections to game previews, match reports, and player profiles. The coverage helped to generate excitement and anticipation for games, drawing in fans who might not have been directly connected to the colleges. The rise of radio broadcasts in the 1920s further expanded the reach of college football, allowing fans across the country to follow their favorite teams and games in real-time.

The popularization of football in colleges was not without its challenges. The increasing commercialization of the sport and the intense pressure on players led to concerns about the impact on academics and the welfare of student-athletes. However, despite these challenges, the sport continued to grow, becoming an integral part of the American collegiate experience.

By the mid-20th century, college football had firmly established itself as a major sport in the United States, with a dedicated fan base, rich traditions, and a deep cultural significance. The roots of this popularity can be traced back to the late 19th and early 20th centuries when football first captured the imagination of college students and the broader public, laying the foundation for the sport's enduring legacy in American culture.

The Emergence of Professional Football

The emergence of professional football in the United States was a gradual and often tumultuous process that began in the late 19th century, eventually evolving into a fully organized and commercialized sport by the early 20th century. Unlike college football, which quickly gained popularity and institutional backing, professional football encountered a series of formidable challenges in its early years. Public skepticism, financial instability, and the absence of a standardized league structure all threatened to undermine the sport's development. Yet, through perseverance, strategic innovation, and the efforts of key individuals, professional football slowly carved out its own niche, laying the crucial groundwork for what would eventually become the National Football League (NFL).

The roots of professional football can be traced back to small towns and industrial cities in Pennsylvania, Ohio, and Illinois, where local athletic clubs and factory teams would frequently compete against each other. These early contests were amateur in nature, reflecting the recreational ethos of the time. However, as the sport grew in popularity, the competitive stakes rose, and players began to receive compensation for their participation. This marked the initial steps toward the professionalization of the game. The first known instance of a player being paid occurred in 1892 when William "Pudge" Heffelfinger, a former Yale star, was paid $500 to play for the Allegheny Athletic Association against the Pittsburgh Athletic Club. This event is often cited as the official birth of professional football, signaling the sport's transition from amateur pastime to a profession.

Despite this early milestone, professional football faced an uphill battle in gaining widespread acceptance. Many in the public viewed the sport as disreputable, associating it with gambling, rough play, and a lack of moral integrity. College football, in contrast, was considered more respectable, enjoying ties to prestigious universities and an emphasis on amateurism that aligned with societal values of the time. However, the demand for competitive football beyond the college level persisted, particularly in working-class communities where the sport provided a valuable source of entertainment and local pride. These communities were instrumental in sustaining professional football during its formative years, despite the broader public's ambivalence.

In its early stages, professional football was characterized by a lack of organization and consistency. Teams were often loosely organized, with no formal league structure to govern the sport. Games were arranged on an ad-hoc basis, with teams playing for little more than local bragging rights. The absence of a consistent schedule and standardized rules made it difficult for the sport to attract a stable fan base or generate significant revenue. Many teams struggled to survive financially, and the sport was marked by frequent team dissolutions and short-lived leagues. However, the competitive nature of the games and the emerging rivalries between teams gradually began to draw attention, slowly building a dedicated following.

The turning point for professional football came in the 1920s, with the formation of the American Professional Football Association (APFA) in 1920. This organization, which was later renamed the National Football League (NFL) in 1922, provided the sport with a much-needed formal organizational structure. The NFL established a regular season schedule, standardized rules, and introduced a championship game to determine the best team each year. These developments helped to legitimize professional football in the eyes of the public and attracted both players and fans who had previously been more interested in the established college game.

The establishment of the NFL marked the beginning of a new era for professional football. Under the guidance of visionary leaders like **George Halas** and **Curly Lambeau**, the league began to expand, moving beyond its regional roots and into larger markets. This expansion was crucial in broadening the league's appeal and securing its financial stability. The introduction of the annual NFL Championship Game in 1933 further solidified the league's legitimacy, giving teams and fans a clear goal to strive toward and helping to create lasting rivalries that fueled the sport's popularity.

By the end of the 1940s, the NFL had firmly established itself as the premier professional football league in the United States. The league's structure, combined with its growing fan base and the increasing popularity of the game, set the stage for the explosive growth and commercial success that would follow in the coming decades. The NFL's emergence as a dominant force in American sports culture was a testament to the resilience and vision of those who had believed in the potential of professional football, even when its future seemed uncertain.

CHAPTER 2: THE BIRTH OF PROFESSIONAL FOOTBALL (1900-1920)

The First Professional Teams

In the early 1900s, professional football in the United States was still in its infancy, with most games played by local athletic clubs and factory teams. These teams were often loosely organized, lacking the formal structure that would later define the sport. However, this period saw the formation of the first professional football teams, laying the groundwork for the sport's evolution into a fully professional league.

One of the earliest professional football teams was the **Latrobe Athletic Association** from Latrobe, Pennsylvania. The team, formed in the late 1890s, became fully professional by 1897 when it paid its players a salary to compete. Latrobe's decision to pay its athletes marked a significant departure from the amateur status that dominated the sport at the time. The team played against other regional teams, drawing local crowds and beginning to establish football as a spectator sport.

Another pioneering team was the **Allegheny Athletic Association**, based in Pittsburgh. The Allegheny team is famously associated with the first documented case of a player being paid to participate in a football game. On November 12, 1892, Allegheny paid William "Pudge" Heffelfinger $500 to play in a game against the Pittsburgh Athletic Club. This event is often cited as the birth of professional football, as it marked the first time a player was openly compensated for their participation, challenging the amateur norms of the sport.

The **Pittsburgh Stars** were another early professional team that were important in the sport's development. Formed in 1902, the Stars competed in the first known professional football league, the National Football League—not to be confused with the modern NFL—which was created by baseball's National League. The Pittsburgh Stars, along with the Philadelphia Athletics and the Pittsburgh Athletic Club, were part of this league. The Stars won the league's only championship in 1902, further solidifying the viability of professional football as a competitive and commercial enterprise.

In Ohio, professional football was taking root in cities like Canton, Akron, and Massillon. The **Massillon Tigers** and the **Canton Bulldogs** became two of the most famous early professional teams. The Massillon Tigers, formed in 1903, quickly established themselves as one of the top teams in the region. They played against local rivals, most notably the Canton Bulldogs, in games that attracted significant attention and large crowds. The rivalry between Massillon and Canton was intense, with the teams often competing for regional supremacy.

The **Canton Bulldogs** were particularly important in the history of professional football. The team was founded in 1905 and became known for its dominance on the field. The Bulldogs were led by Jim Thorpe, one of the most famous athletes of the early 20th century, who joined the team in 1915. Thorpe's presence brought national attention to the Bulldogs and to professional football in general. Under his leadership, the Bulldogs became one of the most successful teams of the era, winning several championships and helping to elevate the status of professional football.

The **Akron Pros**, another Ohio-based team, were established in 1908 and later became a founding member of the American Professional Football Association (APFA), the precursor to the modern NFL, in 1920. The Akron Pros were one of the early teams to formalize the professional nature of the sport, paying their players and competing in a structured league. The team won the first APFA championship in 1920, a significant milestone in the history of professional football.

In addition to these teams, the **Rochester Jeffersons** and the **Rock Island Independents** were among the first professional teams to gain prominence in the Midwest. The Rochester Jeffersons, based in New York, started as a semi-professional team in the early 1900s before turning fully professional. The Rock Island Independents, based in Illinois, were another early professional team that competed in various regional leagues before joining the APFA in 1920.

These early professional teams were instrumental in the development of football as a professional sport. They faced numerous challenges, including financial instability, a lack of formal league structures, and public skepticism. However, their persistence and success on the field helped to establish football as a viable professional sport. The formation of these teams also set the stage for the creation of the American Professional Football Association in 1920, which would later become the National Football League (NFL).

The early professional teams were more than just pioneers; they were the foundation upon which modern professional football was built. Their willingness to innovate and push the boundaries of the sport's amateur traditions laid the groundwork for football's transformation into a national pastime and a major professional league.

The Formation of the Ohio League

The Ohio League, formed in the early 1900s, was a crucial step in the development of professional football in the United States. This loose association of football teams from Ohio and nearby areas laid the foundation for what would eventually become the National Football League (NFL). The Ohio League was not a formal league with a set schedule and centralized governance, but rather a network of teams that played against each other in a highly competitive environment. Despite its informal structure, the Ohio League played a pivotal role in professionalizing the sport and establishing some of its earliest powerhouses.

The Ohio League's origins can be traced back to the increasing popularity of professional football in Ohio's industrial towns, such as Canton, Massillon, and Akron. These towns had strong local teams, many of which began to pay their players by the early 1900s, making them some of the first professional football teams in the country. The formation of the Ohio League provided these teams with a regular schedule of competitive games, attracting large crowds and generating significant local interest.

One of the key features of the Ohio League was the intense rivalry between the **Canton Bulldogs** and the **Massillon Tigers**. This rivalry became the centerpiece of the league, drawing widespread attention and establishing the two teams as the dominant forces in early professional football. The games between Canton and Massillon were hard-fought and often controversial, with allegations of players being poached and disputes over the outcomes of matches. The rivalry reached its peak in the mid-1900s, with the teams competing for the unofficial title of Ohio League champions.

The Ohio League was also notable for its role in attracting some of the top football talent of the time. Players like **Jim Thorpe**, who would later become one of the most famous athletes in American history, played in the Ohio League and helped to raise the profile of professional football. Thorpe, who joined the Canton Bulldogs in 1915, was already a national hero due to his success in the 1912 Olympics, and his involvement in the league brought new levels of attention and legitimacy to the sport.

Despite its success in organizing regular competitive play, the Ohio League faced challenges due to its informal nature. There was no central authority to enforce rules or schedules, leading to disputes and inconsistencies. Teams often played different numbers of games, and there was no standardized method for determining a champion. These issues highlighted the need for a more formal structure to govern professional football, setting the stage for the eventual formation of a national league.

By the late 1910s, the Ohio League began to lose its dominance as other regions, particularly the East Coast and the Midwest, started to develop their own professional teams and leagues. However, the impact of the Ohio League on the development of professional football was undeniable. It provided a proving ground for the sport's early stars and established many of the traditions and rivalries that would carry over into the National Football League.

The Ohio League's legacy lives on in the history of American football. It was a crucial stepping stone in the evolution of the sport, demonstrating the viability of professional football and setting the stage for the creation of a more formalized league system. The teams and players of the Ohio League were pioneers, helping to shape the future of football in the United States and laying the groundwork for the professional game we know today.

The Establishment of the American Professional Football Association (APFA)

The establishment of the American Professional Football Association (APFA) in 1920 marked a turning point in the history of professional football in the United States. The APFA was the first organized league for professional football, providing a formal structure that brought together teams from across the country under a unified set of rules. This organization laid the foundation for what would eventually become the National Football League (NFL), transforming professional football from a loosely organized pastime into a major American sport.

The formation of the APFA was driven by the need to bring order to the chaotic world of early professional football. By the late 1910s, professional teams had sprung up across the country, particularly in the industrial Midwest and East Coast. However, there was no centralized organization to govern the sport, leading to a variety of issues such as inconsistent rules, disputed championships, and the poaching of players between teams. The APFA was created to address these problems by establishing a formal league with standardized rules, schedules, and regulations.

The initial meeting to form the APFA took place on September 17, 1920, at the Jordan and Hupmobile auto showroom in Canton, Ohio. Representatives from 10 teams attended, including the **Akron Pros**, **Canton Bulldogs**, **Cleveland Indians**, and the **Dayton Triangles** from Ohio, as well as teams from New York, Illinois, and Indiana. The meeting was spearheaded by Ralph Hay, the owner of the Canton Bulldogs, who recognized the need for a more organized approach to professional football. During the meeting, the representatives agreed to form the APFA and established a league office in Canton, with Jim Thorpe, one of the most famous athletes of the time, appointed as the first president of the league.

One of the primary goals of the APFA was to establish a standardized schedule and a clear system for determining a champion. In the early years of professional football, teams often played uneven numbers of games, making it difficult to crown a legitimate champion. The APFA sought to remedy this by creating a more uniform schedule and implementing a system where teams would compete for the best overall record. This change brought a new level of legitimacy to professional football, as it introduced a clear pathway to a championship and helped to attract more fans to the sport.

The APFA also introduced a set of standardized rules that all teams were required to follow. This was a significant step forward, as it ensured that all games were played under the same conditions, reducing the confusion and disputes that had plagued the sport in its early years. The league also began to regulate player contracts, addressing the issue of players jumping from team to team, which had been a major problem in the past.

The formation of the APFA was a pivotal moment in the evolution of professional football. It provided the sport with the structure and organization it needed to grow and thrive. The league's first season in 1920 was a modest success, with the Akron Pros emerging as the first champions. Although the league was still in its infancy and faced many challenges, the establishment of the APFA marked the beginning of a new era for professional football.

In 1922, just two years after its formation, the APFA was renamed the National Football League (NFL), a name that would become synonymous with professional football in the United States. The transition from the APFA to the NFL reflected the growing ambition and scope of the league, as it sought to expand its influence and solidify its place in American sports culture.

The creation of the APFA was more than just a response to the disorganization of early professional football; it was the foundation upon which the modern NFL was built. The league's establishment signaled the beginning of professional football as a serious and structured sport, setting the stage for its growth into the national pastime it is today.

Key Early Players and Influencers

The early years of professional football were shaped by a handful of key players and influencers whose contributions helped to define the sport. These individuals were not just athletes but also pioneers who played pivotal roles in establishing football as a legitimate and popular American pastime.

Jim Thorpe stands out as one of the most influential figures in the history of early professional football. Thorpe, a Native American athlete from Oklahoma, was already a sports legend by the time he entered professional football, having won gold medals in the pentathlon and decathlon at the 1912 Olympics. His athleticism and versatility made him a dominant force on the field. Thorpe played for several teams, including the Canton Bulldogs, where he became a symbol of excellence in the sport. Beyond his prowess as a player, Thorpe also served as the first president of the American Professional Football Association (APFA), the precursor to the NFL, lending his fame and credibility to the fledgling league.

Another key figure, introduced earlier, was **Walter Camp**, often referred to as the "Father of American Football." While Camp's direct involvement in professional football was limited, his influence on the game's early development was profound. Camp was instrumental in shaping the rules of the sport, introducing innovations such as the line of scrimmage, the system of downs, and the concept of the quarterback. These changes transformed football from a chaotic, rugby-like game into a structured and strategic sport, laying the foundation for its future as a professional league.

George Halas was another critical figure in the early years of professional football. Halas, a player, coach, and owner, was one of the founding members of the NFL and the longtime owner of the Chicago Bears. His contributions to the game went beyond the field, as he was also a key promoter and marketer of the sport. Halas understood the importance of growing the league's fan base and was instrumental in developing the NFL into a viable business. His innovations, including the introduction of team scouting and the emphasis on physical conditioning, helped to elevate the level of play and professionalism in the league.

Red Grange, known as the "Galloping Ghost," was one of the first football players to achieve national celebrity status. A star at the University of Illinois, Grange brought unprecedented attention to professional football when he joined the Chicago Bears in 1925. His signing was a turning point for the NFL, as it marked the moment when college stars began to transition to the professional game. Grange's popularity and his ability to draw large crowds to games demonstrated the commercial potential of professional football and helped to legitimize the NFL in the eyes of the public.

These early players and influencers were more than just athletes; they were pioneers who helped to shape the sport of football during its formative years. Their contributions laid the groundwork for the development of professional football into a major American sport, influencing the game's rules, structure, and culture in ways that continue to resonate today.

Challenges of Legitimacy and Recognition

In the early 20th century, professional football faced significant challenges in gaining legitimacy and recognition. Unlike college football, which was already well-established and widely respected, professional football was often viewed with skepticism and disdain. Overcoming these challenges was crucial for the sport's survival and growth.

One of the primary challenges was the perception that professional football was a disreputable endeavor. The early professional teams were often associated with rough play, gambling, and a lack of organization, which made it difficult for the sport to be taken seriously. College football, by contrast, was linked to prestigious universities and the ideals of amateurism, which gave it an air of respectability that professional football lacked. As a result, many fans and sportswriters dismissed professional football as a lesser, more commercialized version of the college game.

Another significant challenge was the lack of a centralized league or governing body to standardize the rules and structure of professional football. In the early years, teams operated independently, with no consistent schedule or uniform set of rules. This lack of organization led to chaotic and often controversial games, undermining the sport's credibility. The formation of the American Professional Football Association (APFA) in 1920, which later became the NFL, was a crucial step in addressing this issue. The league provided a framework for regular competition and introduced standardized rules, helping to bring order and legitimacy to professional football.

Financial instability also posed a major challenge to the early professional teams. Many teams struggled to attract large crowds and generate enough revenue to cover expenses, leading to frequent bankruptcies and disbandments. The financial instability was exacerbated by the fact that professional football was still a niche sport, with a relatively small fan base compared to baseball or college football. Teams often had to rely on local support and the dedication of a few wealthy individuals to stay afloat. The creation of a formal league structure, with regular games and championship titles, helped to stabilize the sport financially by increasing its appeal to fans and sponsors.

Public skepticism about the quality of play in professional football was another barrier to legitimacy. College football was seen as the pinnacle of the sport, with the best players and most competitive games. In contrast, professional football was often viewed as a place for players who couldn't succeed in the college ranks. This perception began to change as more college stars, like Red Grange, made the jump to the professional game. The arrival of these high-profile players helped to elevate the standard of play in professional football and attracted more fans, gradually shifting public perception in favor of the professional game.

The early years of professional football were marked by a struggle for legitimacy and recognition. The sport faced numerous challenges, from financial instability to public skepticism, but the efforts to overcome these obstacles were instrumental in laying the groundwork for the NFL's eventual success. The formation of a centralized league, the recruitment of top talent, and the improvement in the quality of play all contributed to the gradual acceptance of professional football as a legitimate and respected sport.

The Role of Early Stadiums and Infrastructure

The development of early stadiums and infrastructure played a critical role in the growth and popularization of professional football. These venues were more than just places to play; they were symbols of the sport's rising status and essential components in creating a sustainable and profitable league.

In the early days of professional football, games were often played in makeshift venues—open fields, high school stadiums, or baseball parks adapted for football. These venues were often ill-suited for the sport, with poor sightlines, inadequate seating, and minimal facilities for players and fans alike. Despite these limitations, early professional teams made do with what was available, but the lack of dedicated football stadiums was a significant hurdle to the sport's growth.

The construction of purpose-built football stadiums in the 1920s marked a turning point in the sport's development. These stadiums provided a more professional and organized environment for games, helping to attract larger crowds and enhance the overall experience for fans. One of the most notable early football stadiums was the **Yale Bowl**, completed in 1914. Although primarily used for college football, the Yale Bowl set a new standard for football venues with its large seating capacity and modern facilities. It demonstrated the potential for football-specific stadiums to draw significant crowds and generate substantial revenue.

As professional football began to gain traction, teams started to invest in their own stadiums. The **Chicago Bears**, for example, played in Wrigley Field, a baseball park, but began to seek a more suitable venue as their popularity grew. The Bears' eventual move to Soldier Field in 1926, a stadium with a much larger capacity, reflected the team's rising status and the increasing demand for professional football. The move to larger and more modern stadiums allowed teams to accommodate more fans, generate more income from ticket sales, and create a more exciting game-day atmosphere.

The rise of early stadiums also was important in the marketing and promotion of professional football. A well-located and well-designed stadium could become a landmark in its city, helping to build a team's identity and attract a loyal fan base. Teams began to recognize the importance of creating a strong connection with their local communities, using their stadiums as a focal point for civic pride and local support. This connection was particularly important in smaller industrial towns, where the local football team often served as a source of entertainment and community identity.

The infrastructure surrounding these early stadiums also evolved to support the growing popularity of the sport. Improved transportation, such as streetcars and later automobiles, made it easier for fans to travel to games, expanding the potential audience beyond those who lived within walking distance of the stadium. The introduction of lighting for night games in the late 1920s further expanded the reach of professional football, allowing teams to play games outside of traditional working hours and attracting larger crowds.

The development of early stadiums and infrastructure was a key factor in the growth of professional football. These investments not only provided the necessary facilities for the sport to flourish but also helped to elevate its status and appeal to a broader audience. The early stadiums were more than just venues; they were symbols of the sport's potential and was important in its transformation into a major American pastime.

CHAPTER 3: THE NFL IS BORN (1920S)

Transition from APFA to NFL

The transition from the American Professional Football Association (APFA) to the National Football League (NFL) in the 1920s was a pivotal moment in the history of American football. This shift marked the beginning of a more organized and professional era for the sport, setting the stage for the NFL to become the powerhouse it is today.

The APFA was formed in 1920, bringing together a collection of regional football teams under a single umbrella. The goal was to create a more structured environment for professional football, with standardized rules, schedules, and a system for determining a champion. The league started with 14 teams, mostly from the Midwest, including the Akron Pros, Canton Bulldogs, Decatur Staleys, and Chicago Cardinals. From the beginning, the APFA sought to bring legitimacy to professional football, which had long been overshadowed by the more established and respected college game.

One of the key figures in this transition was **Ralph Hay**, the owner of the Canton Bulldogs and the driving force behind the formation of the APFA. Hay recognized the need for a more organized league to stabilize the sport and reduce the chaos that had plagued professional football in its early years. He used his auto dealership in Canton, Ohio, as the venue for the league's first meetings, where representatives from various teams gathered to lay the groundwork for what would become the NFL.

The initial years of the APFA were marked by a struggle for survival and legitimacy. Teams came and went, and the league faced significant financial challenges. However, the league began to find its footing, thanks in large part to the leadership of Jim Thorpe, the APFA's first president, who was also one of the most famous athletes in the country. Thorpe's involvement brought much-needed attention and credibility to the fledgling league.

In 1922, just two years after its formation, the APFA was renamed the National Football League (NFL). This name change was more than just a rebranding; it signaled the league's ambition to become the dominant force in professional football across the United States. The new name also reflected the league's growing geographical reach, as it sought to expand beyond its Midwestern roots and attract teams from across the country.

The transition to the NFL was accompanied by several important changes that helped to solidify the league's structure and position in the sports world. One of the most significant developments was the introduction of a more formalized schedule and championship system. The league moved away from the irregular and often chaotic scheduling of the APFA years, where teams played varying numbers of games, to a more organized approach where each team played a set schedule. This change made the competition more predictable and helped to build excitement among fans as teams competed for a clear championship title.

Another key factor in the NFL's early success was the emergence of strong, stable franchises that would become the bedrock of the league. Teams like the **Chicago Bears** (originally the Decatur Staleys) and the **Green Bay Packers** began to establish themselves as perennial contenders, building loyal fan bases and creating the rivalries that would become central to the NFL's appeal. The stability of these teams, along with the league's efforts to enforce financial discipline among its members, helped to create a more sustainable model for professional football.

The NFL also benefited from the rise of star players who captured the public's imagination. Players like **Red Grange**, who joined the Chicago Bears in 1925, brought national attention to the league. Grange's signing was a turning point for the NFL, as it demonstrated the league's ability to attract top talent and compete with college football for the best players. His success on the field and his ability to draw large crowds helped to boost the NFL's profile and solidify its place in American sports.

By the end of the 1920s, the NFL had established itself as the premier professional football league in the United States. The transition from the APFA to the NFL was a critical step in this process, providing the organizational structure, stability, and national reach that the sport needed to grow and thrive. This period laid the foundation for the NFL's future success, setting the stage for it to become the dominant force in American sports that it is today.

Early NFL Teams and Founding Members

The early years of the National Football League (NFL) were shaped by a mix of teams, some of which remain iconic franchises today, while others have faded into history. The league's formation in 1920 brought together a group of teams that would lay the foundation for professional football in the United States.

Among the 14 original teams that joined the NFL, then known as the American Professional Football Association (APFA), were the **Akron Pros**, **Canton Bulldogs**, **Decatur Staleys**, and **Chicago Cardinals**. The Akron Pros, led by coach Fritz Pollard, were the first team to win an NFL championship, going undefeated in the league's inaugural season. Their success set a high standard for competition in the early years of the league.

The **Canton Bulldogs**, another key founding team, were already a well-established football club before the NFL's formation. Known for their intense rivalry with the Massillon Tigers during their Ohio League days, the Bulldogs became a dominant force in the early NFL. The Bulldogs, with star player Jim Thorpe, one of the most famous athletes of the time, were instrumental in bringing national attention to the league.

The **Decatur Staleys**, founded by the A.E. Staley Company, were one of the most important early franchises. Coached by George Halas, the Staleys moved to Chicago in 1921 and were renamed the Chicago Bears the following year. The Bears would go on to become one of the most storied franchises in NFL history, known for their tough, defensive style of play.

The **Chicago Cardinals** (now the Arizona Cardinals) were another original member of the NFL. Although the team struggled in its early years, the Cardinals have the distinction of being the oldest continuously run professional football team in the United States, having been founded in 1898 as the Morgan Athletic Club.

Other original teams included the **Dayton Triangles**, **Rochester Jeffersons**, and **Rock Island Independents**. These teams contributed to the league's early growth but eventually folded or merged with other franchises as the NFL expanded and evolved.

The league's founding members were united by their desire to bring organization and legitimacy to professional football, which had previously been a chaotic and financially unstable sport. These early teams were important in establishing the NFL's identity and laying the groundwork for the league's future success.

Though not all of the original teams survived, their contributions to the NFL's early years were vital. They helped to create a competitive environment that would attract fans, players, and media attention, ultimately transforming the NFL into a major force in American sports.

The Role of George Halas

George Halas, often referred to as "Papa Bear," was one of the most influential figures in the history of the National Football League (NFL). His impact on the league extended far beyond his role as a player and coach; Halas was a visionary who helped shape the NFL into the powerhouse it is today.

Halas's journey in professional football began with the **Decatur Staleys**, a team sponsored by the A.E. Staley Company in 1919. Halas was hired as a player-coach, and his leadership quickly became evident. In 1921, Halas moved the team to Chicago, renaming them the Chicago Bears. This move was a pivotal moment in

NFL history, as it established the Bears as one of the league's cornerstone franchises.

As a coach, Halas was known for his innovative approach to the game. He emphasized physical conditioning and introduced new strategies that would become staples of the sport. One of his most significant contributions was the development of the T-formation offense, which revolutionized football by placing the quarterback under center and utilizing a more dynamic running and passing attack. This strategy not only led the Bears to multiple championships but also influenced the way football was played across the league.

Beyond his contributions on the field, Halas was instrumental in the business side of the NFL. He understood the importance of marketing and fan engagement, helping to grow the league's popularity. Halas was also a key figure in the establishment of the NFL's revenue-sharing model, which helped ensure the financial stability of all teams in the league, not just the most successful ones. This model was crucial in fostering a competitive balance that allowed the NFL to thrive.

Halas's influence extended to the broader NFL community. He was a founding member of the league and served on various committees that shaped the NFL's rules and policies. His commitment to the league was unwavering; he coached the Bears for an incredible 40 seasons, amassing a then-record 318 wins. Under his leadership, the Bears won eight NFL championships, solidifying his legacy as one of the greatest coaches in the history of the sport.

George Halas's impact on the NFL cannot be overstated. He was a pioneer who helped turn a fledgling league into a national institution. His innovations on the field, combined with his business acumen and dedication to the sport, played a critical role in shaping the NFL's early success and ensuring its long-term growth. Halas's legacy lives on not only in the history books but also in the continued success of the Chicago Bears and the NFL as a whole.

The NFL's Struggles in the Early Years

The National Football League (NFL) faced significant struggles during its early years, fighting for survival in a landscape dominated by other sports, particularly college football and baseball. From financial instability to public skepticism, the league's early years were marked by challenges that threatened its very existence.

When the NFL was first established as the American Professional Football Association (APFA) in 1920, it consisted of a collection of loosely organized teams, many of which operated on shoestring budgets. The league lacked the stability and credibility that fans associated with college football, which had already established itself as a prestigious and respected sport. Professional football, by contrast, was often seen as a lower-tier, rough-and-tumble alternative that struggled to attract a loyal following.

Financial instability was one of the most pressing issues for the early NFL. Many teams operated in small industrial towns with limited resources, relying heavily on gate receipts to stay afloat. Attendance was inconsistent, and the lack of lucrative sponsorship deals or media contracts made it difficult for teams to generate the revenue needed to cover expenses. As a result, teams frequently folded or relocated, creating an unstable environment that made it difficult for the league to build a consistent fan base.

Another challenge was the league's struggle to maintain a standardized schedule and set of rules. The early NFL was plagued by a lack of organization, with teams often playing uneven numbers of games, leading to disputes over championship titles. This lack of structure undermined the league's credibility and made it difficult to attract serious attention from sportswriters and the general public. Without a clear, organized competition, the NFL struggled to compete with the well-established traditions of college football, which had a more coherent and respected structure.

Public perception was another significant hurdle. In the 1920s, the idea of professional athletes was still relatively new, and there was a widespread belief that sports should remain amateur. This belief was particularly strong in college football, which was seen as a purer form of the game. The professional players were often viewed with suspicion, and the NFL struggled to gain the same level of respect and admiration that college teams enjoyed. This perception made it difficult for the NFL to attract top talent, as many of the best players preferred to stay in the college ranks or pursue other careers.

Despite these struggles, the NFL managed to survive its early years through the perseverance of its teams and the leadership of key figures like George Halas and Jim Thorpe. The league slowly began to gain traction, setting the stage for future growth. However, the challenges of the early years left a lasting impact on the NFL, shaping its development and the strategies it would use to eventually become a dominant force in American sports.

Popularity Compared to Baseball

In the early 20th century, baseball reigned supreme as America's pastime, far outstripping football in terms of popularity, media attention, and cultural significance. The NFL, founded in 1920, struggled to gain a foothold in a sports landscape dominated by baseball, which had become deeply entrenched in American culture by the time professional football was just getting started.

Baseball's popularity was built on a foundation of history and tradition. By the 1920s, Major League Baseball (MLB) had been around for over half a century, with legendary players like Babe Ruth and Ty Cobb becoming household names. The sport was a source of national pride and a symbol of American identity, with its leisurely pace and summer-long season appealing to a broad audience. Baseball games were a social event, drawing large crowds and receiving extensive coverage in newspapers and on the radio. In contrast, the NFL, with its rough-and-tumble image and less-established teams, struggled to attract similar attention.

The structure of baseball also contributed to its popularity. Major League Baseball was well-organized, with clearly defined leagues, a stable schedule, and a World Series that captured the public's imagination each year. In contrast, the NFL's early years were marked by disorganization, with teams often playing uneven schedules and championships decided through informal agreements rather than a playoff system. This lack of structure made it difficult for professional football to build the same level of fan engagement and excitement that baseball enjoyed.

Baseball's dominance was also reflected in the media. Newspapers devoted pages to baseball coverage, and radio broadcasts brought the game into the homes of millions of Americans. Baseball players were celebrated as national heroes, and their exploits on the field were followed by fans across the country. Football, on the other hand, was still fighting for recognition. The NFL's games were often overshadowed by college football, which was seen as a more prestigious and respectable version of the sport. Professional football players did not receive the same level of acclaim, and the NFL struggled to break into the national conversation.

Despite these challenges, football's physicality and the shorter, more intense season began to attract a different kind of fan. The NFL's games were faster-paced and more brutal than baseball, offering a different type of excitement. As the league grew and the quality of play improved, football started to carve out its niche, particularly in the colder months when baseball was off-season. However, throughout the 1920s, baseball remained the undisputed king of American sports, with football only beginning to lay the groundwork for its eventual rise.

The popularity gap between baseball and football in the early 20th century highlights the challenges the NFL faced in its quest to become a major sport. While baseball had the advantage of tradition, organization, and media support, football's appeal lay in its intensity and the burgeoning rivalries that would eventually capture the American imagination.

The Red Grange Impact

The arrival of Harold "Red" Grange in professional football marked a turning point in the NFL's history, bringing unprecedented attention and legitimacy to the league. The "Galloping Ghost" was one of the most famous college football players of his time, and his decision to turn professional in 1925 had a profound impact on the sport.

Red Grange's college career at the University of Illinois was nothing short of legendary. His combination of speed, agility, and football intelligence made him a star, and his performances drew national attention. In an era when college football was far more popular than its professional counterpart, Grange was seen as the epitome of what a football player should be. His decision to join the Chicago Bears just days after his final college game was a bold move that sent shockwaves through the sports world.

When Grange signed with the Chicago Bears, it was a watershed moment for the NFL. At the time, professional football struggled to attract top talent, as many players preferred the prestige and stability of college football or pursued other careers. Grange's move to the NFL instantly legitimized the league in the eyes of the public and the media. For the first time, a marquee college player had chosen the professional ranks, and this decision helped to shift perceptions about the NFL.

Grange's impact on the field was immediate. His debut with the Bears on Thanksgiving Day in 1925 drew a record crowd, and his subsequent performances on a grueling nationwide barnstorming tour packed stadiums across the country. Fans flocked to see the "Galloping Ghost" in action, and his presence on the Bears' roster brought a level of excitement and media coverage that the NFL had never experienced before. The tour, organized by Bears owner George Halas, was a financial success, generating significant revenue and exposing professional football to new audiences in cities across America.

Beyond his contributions on the field, Grange's decision to turn professional had a lasting impact on the NFL's business model. His signing demonstrated that the league could attract top talent and compete with college football for the best players. This helped to raise the overall level of play in the NFL and made the league more appealing to fans and sponsors. Grange's popularity also showed that professional football could be a viable career for athletes, encouraging more college stars to consider joining the NFL.

Red Grange's influence extended far beyond his playing days. He helped to bridge the gap between college and professional football, paving the way for the NFL to grow into a major sports league. His decision to join the NFL was a defining moment in the league's history, and his legacy as one of the game's first true superstars remains an integral part of the NFL's story. Grange's impact demonstrated the potential of professional football, setting the stage for the NFL's future success and its eventual rise to prominence in American sports.

CHAPTER 4: THE 1930S - SURVIVAL AND GROWTH

The NFL's Financial Struggles During the Great Depression

The 1930s were a decade of immense challenge for the National Football League (NFL), as the Great Depression cast a long shadow over the United States. The economic hardships of the era hit professional sports hard, and the NFL was no exception. As businesses closed and unemployment soared, the league struggled to stay afloat, facing financial difficulties that threatened its very existence.

The Great Depression began with the stock market crash of 1929, which led to widespread economic instability. For the NFL, this meant declining attendance at games, as many fans could no longer afford the price of a ticket. Football was a luxury that few could justify when basic necessities were a struggle to secure. The financial strain on the league was immediate and severe, with teams across the country feeling the impact. **Gate receipts**, the primary source of revenue for NFL teams, plummeted, forcing franchises to operate on razor-thin margins.

Many teams in the NFL were small operations with limited financial backing, and the Depression exposed the fragility of these organizations. Several teams folded during the early 1930s, unable to withstand the financial pressures. The **Portsmouth Spartans, Cleveland Indians**, and **Brooklyn Dodgers** were among those that either disbanded or were forced to relocate due to financial instability. Even established teams like the Chicago Bears and Green Bay Packers struggled to stay solvent, relying heavily on the dedication and personal finances of their owners to survive.

The financial difficulties of the Depression also forced the NFL to get creative in its efforts to attract fans. Teams began to experiment with promotional events and lower ticket prices to bring people through the gates. The league also shortened its season and reduced player salaries, understanding that survival required drastic measures. The **Chicago Bears**, for example, introduced innovative marketing strategies, including the use of doubleheaders, where two games were played back-to-back, offering more value to fans and helping to boost attendance.

Despite these efforts, the NFL's struggles continued throughout the 1930s. The league was also competing with college football, which remained more popular with the American public. College teams drew larger crowds, and the college game was seen as more prestigious, further complicating the NFL's efforts to grow during this challenging period. The NFL had to work hard to carve out its niche, emphasizing the higher level of competition and the appeal of professional athletes to draw fans away from the college game.

The financial strain also affected the quality of play on the field. Teams had to cut costs, which often meant reducing the number of players on the roster and cutting back on training and facilities. Injuries were common, and the overall level of play suffered as teams struggled to maintain a full lineup. The Depression era was marked by tough, grinding football, with a focus on defense and conservative play-calling, reflecting the cautious approach teams had to take in such uncertain times.

However, the league did manage to achieve some growth during the 1930s, despite the economic challenges. The introduction of the NFL draft in 1936 was a significant step forward, providing a more equitable way for teams to acquire talent and helping to balance competition across the league. This innovation helped to keep the league competitive and maintained fan interest, even as the nation struggled through the Depression.

The NFL's survival during the Great Depression was a testament to the resilience of the league and its teams. While the decade was undoubtedly difficult, the lessons learned during this period—about financial management, innovation, and the importance of a strong organizational structure—helped to lay the foundation for the NFL's future growth. The struggles of the 1930s forced the NFL to become more professional, more organized, and more determined to succeed, setting the stage for the league's eventual rise to prominence in American sports.

Introduction of the NFL Draft

The introduction of the NFL Draft in 1936 was a groundbreaking moment in the history of professional football. This new system fundamentally changed the way teams acquired talent and helped to level the playing field across the league. Before the draft, NFL teams competed fiercely for top college players, often resulting in wealthier teams securing the best talent, leaving weaker teams struggling to compete. The draft was designed to address this imbalance and ensure that all teams had a fair shot at building a competitive roster.

The idea for the draft came from **Bert Bell**, the co-owner of the Philadelphia Eagles. Bell recognized that the existing system was unsustainable for the league's long-term success. The richer teams, like the New York Giants and Chicago Bears, consistently signed the best players, while teams like Bell's Eagles languished at the bottom of the standings. Bell proposed a draft system where teams would select players in reverse order of their performance from the previous season, with the weakest teams picking first. This idea was revolutionary, and it was quickly adopted by the NFL owners.

The first NFL Draft was held on February 8, 1936, at the Ritz-Carlton Hotel in Philadelphia. There were no elaborate scouting departments or televised events like today; instead, teams relied on limited information about the players. The first player ever selected in the NFL Draft was **Jay Berwanger**, a halfback from the University of Chicago, who was chosen by the Philadelphia Eagles. However, Berwanger never played in the NFL, as he chose to pursue other career opportunities instead. This highlighted the uncertainty and challenges of the early drafts, where teams often had little control over whether a player would actually sign with them.

Despite these early challenges, the NFL Draft quickly became a central component of the league's competitive balance. The draft allowed weaker teams to rebuild by acquiring top college talent, which in turn helped to keep the league competitive and exciting for fans. Over time, the draft process became more sophisticated, with teams investing in scouting and player evaluation to make more informed selections.

The introduction of the NFL Draft was a crucial step in the evolution of the league. It not only provided a more equitable system for distributing talent but also contributed to the growth and stability of the NFL. The draft became an annual event that generated excitement and anticipation among fans, setting the stage for the modern NFL, where the draft remains one of the most important and celebrated events of the year.

The Birth of the Chicago Bears Dynasty

The Chicago Bears emerged as one of the dominant forces in the NFL during the 1940s, establishing a dynasty that would leave a lasting legacy in professional football. The seeds of this dominance were sown in the 1930s under the leadership of **George Halas**, the team's founder, coach, and owner, who played a pivotal role in transforming the Bears into a powerhouse.

The Bears' success was built on a combination of innovative strategy, exceptional talent, and a relentless drive to win. One of the key factors in the birth of the Bears dynasty was Halas's introduction of the T-formation offense, which revolutionized the way football was played. The T-formation, which positioned the quarterback under center with three running backs behind him, allowed for a more versatile and deceptive offense. This formation gave the Bears a significant strategic advantage, making their offense difficult to predict and defend against. The T-formation became the foundation of the Bears' success and was widely adopted across the league.

Another critical element in the Bears' rise to dominance was the acquisition of star players who would become legends of the game. **Sid Luckman**, a quarterback known for his leadership and passing ability, was the perfect fit for Halas's T-formation. Luckman, who joined the Bears in 1939, quickly became the centerpiece of the Bears' offense, leading the team to four NFL championships during his career. His ability to execute the T-formation with precision made the Bears' offense one of the most potent in the league.

The Bears' defense was equally formidable, earning the team the nickname "Monsters of the Midway." Led by standout players like **Bronko Nagurski** and **Bill George**, the Bears' defense was known for its toughness and physicality, consistently shutting down opposing offenses and making Chicago a feared opponent. The combination of a high-powered offense and a stifling defense made the Bears one of the most well-rounded and dominant teams of the era.

The culmination of the Bears' dominance came in the 1940 NFL Championship Game, where they delivered one of the most lopsided victories in football history, defeating the Washington Redskins 73-0. This game, often referred to as the "Perfect Game," showcased the full power of Halas's T-formation and solidified the Bears' place in NFL history. The victory was a statement of the Bears' superiority and set the tone for the team's continued success throughout the 1940s.

The birth of the Chicago Bears dynasty in the late 1930s and early 1940s marked a defining era in NFL history. Under George Halas's leadership, the Bears not only dominated the league but also helped to shape the future of football with their innovative strategies and exceptional play. The Bears' success during this period laid the groundwork for the team's enduring legacy as one of the NFL's most storied franchises.

The First NFL Championship Game

The first NFL Championship Game, played on December 17, 1933, marked a significant milestone in the history of professional football. This game not only crowned the first official league champion under the NFL's new playoff system but also showcased the evolving nature of the sport, particularly in terms of strategy and entertainment value.

Prior to 1933, the NFL determined its champion based solely on the best regular-season record, which often led to disputes and confusion. The 1932 season, for instance, ended with a tie between the Chicago Bears and the Portsmouth Spartans, leading to an impromptu playoff game that the Bears won. This game's success in terms of fan interest and revenue convinced NFL leadership that a structured championship game could be a valuable addition to the league. As a result, the NFL reorganized into two divisions for the 1933 season, with the winners of each division meeting in a championship game to determine the league champion.

The first NFL Championship Game featured the **Chicago Bears** and the **New York Giants**, two of the league's most prominent teams. The game was played at Wrigley Field in Chicago, home of the Bears. The matchup was highly anticipated, as it brought together two teams with contrasting styles— the Bears were known for their powerful running game and the innovative T-formation offense, while the Giants were celebrated for their strong defense and strategic play.

The game lived up to its billing as a showcase of the NFL's growing strategic complexity. The Bears, led by coach George Halas, utilized the T-formation to great effect, with quarterback Bronko Nagurski playing a key role in their offensive attack. The Giants, coached by **Steve Owen**, countered with a tough, disciplined defense that sought to stifle the Bears' running game. The game was a back-and-forth affair, with both teams exchanging the lead multiple times.

In the end, the Bears emerged victorious with a 23-21 win, thanks in part to a trick play where Nagurski faked a run and threw a game-winning touchdown pass to **Bill Hewitt**. This game-winning play was a perfect example of the kind of strategic innovation that was becoming more common in the NFL, as teams began to experiment with new ways to gain an advantage over their opponents.

The success of the first NFL Championship Game cemented the importance of a playoff system in professional football. It provided a clear and exciting conclusion to the season, generating significant interest from fans and the media. The game's popularity ensured that the NFL Championship Game would become an annual tradition, eventually evolving into the Super Bowl, which is now one of the biggest sporting events in the world.

Innovations in the Passing Game

The evolution of the passing game in professional football was one of the most significant developments in the sport's history. While the early years of football were dominated by running plays, the introduction and subsequent innovations in the passing game transformed the way football was played, making it a more dynamic and exciting sport.

In the 1930s and 1940s, the NFL saw a series of key innovations that elevated the passing game from a secondary option to a central element of offensive strategy. One of the most important figures in this transformation was **Sammy Baugh**, a quarterback for the Washington Redskins who revolutionized the way the passing game was approached. Baugh's accuracy, arm strength, and ability to read defenses made him one of the first true passing specialists in the NFL. His impact was profound, as he demonstrated that a strong passing game could be just as effective, if not more so, than a dominant running game.

The introduction of the T formation by **George Halas** and the Chicago Bears also was important in the development of the passing game. The T-formation positioned the quarterback directly behind the center, allowing for quicker and more varied passing plays. This formation provided teams with greater flexibility, enabling them to incorporate short, medium, and long-range passes into their offensive strategies. The T-formation's success, particularly during the Bears' 1940s dynasty, encouraged other teams to adopt and adapt the formation, leading to a league-wide emphasis on more sophisticated passing attacks.

Another significant innovation was the development of the forward pass protection schemes. As the passing game became more central to offensive strategies, teams realized the importance of protecting the quarterback from the increasingly aggressive defenses. Offensive lines began to specialize in pass blocking, and coaches developed new schemes to give quarterbacks more time to find open receivers. This focus on protecting the passer allowed for more complex passing plays, including the use of multiple receivers and more intricate route combinations.

The forward pass itself continued to evolve, with coaches and players experimenting with different techniques to maximize its effectiveness. **Sid Luckman**, another standout quarterback for the Chicago Bears, helped popularize the concept of play-action passing, where the quarterback fakes a handoff to draw the defense in before throwing the ball downfield. This tactic added a new layer of deception to the game and became a staple of NFL offenses.

By the end of the 1940s, the passing game had firmly established itself as a key component of NFL offenses. The innovations introduced during this period laid the groundwork for the modern passing game, which has become the centerpiece of most NFL offenses. The emphasis on passing not only changed the way the game was played but also made football more exciting for fans, with big plays and high-scoring games becoming more common.

The Introduction of the Forward Pass

The introduction of the forward pass in American football was a revolutionary change that fundamentally altered the nature of the game. Before its legalization, football was primarily a ground-based sport, heavily influenced by its rugby origins. The forward pass introduced a new dimension to the game, allowing teams to advance the ball through the air, which opened up the field and made the game faster and more dynamic.

The forward pass was first officially allowed in 1906, as part of a series of rule changes aimed at reducing the violence and injuries that had plagued the sport. Football at the time was brutal, with mass formations like the "flying wedge" leading to numerous injuries and fatalities. The push for reform, led by figures such as President Theodore Roosevelt, resulted in the introduction of several new rules, including the forward pass, which was intended to spread out the players and reduce the frequency of dangerous pile-ups.

However, the early years of the forward pass were marked by caution and uncertainty. Coaches and players were initially reluctant to embrace the new tactic, as the rules governing the pass were still restrictive. For example, the ball had to be thrown from at least five yards behind the line of scrimmage, and an incomplete pass resulted in a turnover. These restrictions made the forward pass a risky proposition, and many teams preferred to stick to the more familiar running game.

Despite these challenges, the forward pass began to gain traction, particularly in college football, where innovative coaches like **Knute Rockne** of Notre Dame saw its potential. Rockne, along with his star player **George Gipp**, used the forward pass to great effect, leading Notre Dame to several successful seasons. The success of Notre Dame's passing game demonstrated the potential of the forward pass and helped to popularize its use across the country.

In the NFL, the forward pass gradually became more accepted as teams realized its strategic value. The league's early pioneers, such as **Curly Lambeau** of the Green Bay Packers and **Sammy Baugh** of the Washington Redskins, began to incorporate the forward pass into their offensive schemes. Baugh, in particular, became one of the first quarterbacks to fully exploit the possibilities of the forward pass, setting numerous passing records and leading the Redskins to multiple championships.

The forward pass also led to significant changes in the way football was played and coached. Offensive strategies became more complex, with teams developing specialized passing plays and route combinations to take advantage of the new rules. Defenses, in turn, had to adapt by developing new coverage schemes and pass-rushing techniques to counter the growing threat of the aerial attack.

The introduction of the forward pass was a turning point in the evolution of football. It transformed the sport from a grinding, ground-based contest into a more open and dynamic game, paving the way for the high-scoring, pass-heavy offenses that dominate the NFL today. The forward pass not only changed the way the game was played but also made football more exciting and accessible to fans, helping to propel the sport to new heights of popularity.

CHAPTER 5: WORLD WAR II AND THE NFL (1940S)

The Impact of the War on the NFL

World War II had a profound impact on the NFL, affecting every aspect of the league, from player rosters to game schedules. The war years were a time of uncertainty and adaptation as the NFL, like the rest of the country, grappled with the demands of a global conflict.

One of the most immediate effects of the war was the depletion of NFL rosters. As young men across the United States enlisted or were drafted into the military, many of the league's star players left to serve. Over 600 NFL players, coaches, and personnel joined the armed forces, including some of the league's biggest names like **Sid Luckman, Chuck Bednarik**, and **Otto Graham**. This mass exodus left teams scrambling to fill their rosters, leading to a significant drop in the quality of play. Many teams had to rely on older players, those classified as unfit for military service, or players from semi-professional teams to field a full squad. The resulting games were often uneven, with mismatched talent levels and a noticeable decline in the level of competition.

The war also forced the NFL to become more flexible with its operations. Some teams faced such severe personnel shortages that they were unable to field a competitive team. In response, the league allowed for temporary mergers between struggling franchises. The most famous of these was the **"Steagles,"** a combination of the Philadelphia Eagles and the Pittsburgh Steelers during the 1943 season. This merger was born out of necessity, as neither team could muster enough players on their own. Despite the challenges, the Steagles managed to post a respectable 5-4-1 record, illustrating the resilience of the teams and the league during this difficult period.

Financially, the NFL faced significant challenges as well. With many games played in front of smaller crowds due to travel restrictions and wartime rationing, revenue streams were severely impacted. Teams struggled to cover operational costs, and some faced the possibility of folding. The league's leadership, under Commissioner Elmer Layden, worked hard to keep the NFL afloat, implementing cost-cutting measures and relying on the loyalty of die-hard fans to sustain the league through these tough times.

Despite these difficulties, the NFL managed to continue its operations throughout the war, providing a sense of normalcy and entertainment for fans on the home front. The league also made efforts to support the war effort directly. NFL games were used as venues for war bond drives, raising funds to support the military.

Players who were not in the service often participated in exhibitions and other events to boost morale and contribute to the war effort.

The end of the war brought about a period of reflection and rebuilding for the NFL. Many of the league's stars returned from military service, and the NFL began to recover from the strains of the war years. The lessons learned during this period of adversity, such as the importance of flexibility and the ability to adapt to changing circumstances, helped to strengthen the league in the years that followed.

The impact of World War II on the NFL was profound, forcing the league to adapt in ways that were unprecedented. Yet, the league's survival during this time demonstrated its resilience and laid the groundwork for its post-war growth, setting the stage for the NFL to become the dominant force in American sports.

The NFL's Wartime Teams and Roster Challenges

During World War II, the NFL faced significant challenges as the war effort drew many of its players, coaches, and staff into military service. The resulting personnel shortages forced the league to adapt quickly, leading to some of the most unusual and challenging seasons in its history.

As the war progressed, over 600 NFL players left to serve in the armed forces. This mass exodus left teams struggling to fill their rosters. The league, desperate to maintain operations, had to be creative in finding replacements. Teams turned to older players, those classified as 4-F (unfit for military service), and even players from semi-professional leagues to keep their rosters full. The talent pool was thin, leading to a noticeable decline in the quality of play across the league. Games often featured mismatched teams, with a few experienced veterans playing alongside less skilled or out-of-practice players.

Another temporary merger occurred in 1944 when the Pittsburgh Steelers combined with the **Chicago Cardinals** to form **Card-Pitt** (often derisively referred to as the "Carpets" due to their poor performance). This team struggled significantly, finishing the season without a single win. The challenges faced by these combined teams highlighted the difficulties of maintaining competitive balance and the strain the war placed on the league.

The war also forced teams to play with shortened rosters, sometimes with as few as 25 players. Coaches had to be flexible, often assigning players to multiple positions to cover gaps. The result was a rugged, no-frills style of football that emphasized survival over strategy. Injuries were common, and teams often had to make do with whatever players were available.

Despite these challenges, the NFL's wartime teams demonstrated remarkable resilience. The league managed to complete its seasons, providing a source of entertainment and a sense of continuity for fans on the home front. The experiences of the wartime teams underscored the NFL's ability to adapt under pressure, laying the groundwork for the league's post-war recovery and growth.

Post-War NFL Expansion

The end of World War II marked the beginning of a new era for the NFL, characterized by significant expansion and growth. As soldiers returned home and the nation shifted its focus from wartime efforts to peacetime prosperity, the NFL seized the opportunity to expand its reach and solidify its place in American sports.

One of the first signs of this post-war expansion was the return of many star players who had served in the military. These athletes, including names like **Otto Graham** and **Chuck Bednarik**, brought renewed energy and skill to the league. Their return helped to elevate the quality of play and drew larger crowds to games, as fans were eager to see their heroes back on the field. The influx of talent also made the league more competitive, as teams worked to build rosters that could contend for championships in this new era.

The NFL also began to expand geographically during this period. In 1946, the league welcomed the **Cleveland Browns** and the **San Francisco 49ers** from the All-America Football Conference (AAFC). These teams brought new markets and fan bases into the NFL fold, helping to grow the league's national footprint. The inclusion of these teams also marked the beginning of a more unified and stable professional football landscape, as the NFL worked to consolidate its position as the premier football league in the United States.

Another significant development was the 1949 merger with the AAFC, which further expanded the league and brought in additional teams like the **Baltimore Colts**. This merger was a strategic move that eliminated competition between the two leagues and strengthened the NFL's position as the dominant force in professional football. The expanded league now had more teams, more games, and a broader national presence, setting the stage for its future growth.

The post-war era also saw innovations in the way the NFL operated. The league began to embrace new media opportunities, with games being broadcast on radio and, increasingly, on television. This exposure helped to bring the NFL into the homes of millions of Americans, further increasing its popularity and fan base.

The NFL's post-war expansion was a critical period in the league's history. The return of star players, the geographic expansion, and the strategic merger with the AAFC all contributed to the NFL's transformation from a regional league into a national powerhouse. This period laid the foundation for the NFL's continued growth and its emergence as one of the most popular sports leagues in the world.

The Birth of the Cleveland Browns

The Cleveland Browns were born out of the ambition and vision of **Paul Brown**, one of the most influential figures in football history. Founded in 1944 as part of the newly formed All-America Football Conference (AAFC), the Browns quickly became one of the most dominant teams in professional football, setting a standard of excellence that would resonate throughout the sport.

Paul Brown, already a highly respected coach due to his success at Massillon High School and Ohio State University, was recruited by businessman **Arthur "Mickey" McBride** to lead Cleveland's new professional football team. Brown brought with him a revolutionary approach to coaching and team management, emphasizing organization, preparation, and the use of playbooks—concepts that were relatively new to professional football at the time. His methods, which included detailed scouting, rigorous practices, and innovative strategies, would soon pay dividends on the field.

The team was named the Cleveland Browns after a public contest, although Brown himself was initially hesitant to have the team named after him. Despite his reluctance, the name stuck, and it wasn't long before the Browns began to make their mark on the AAFC. The Browns' roster was built with a mix of experienced players and young talent, many of whom were handpicked by Paul Brown. One of the most notable acquisitions was quarterback **Otto Graham**, who would become a central figure in the team's success.

From the very beginning, the Browns dominated the AAFC. In their inaugural season in 1946, they posted a 12-2 record, showcasing a powerful offense and a stingy defense. The team was particularly known for its precision and discipline, hallmarks of Paul Brown's coaching style. The Browns' offensive strategy, centered around Graham's passing ability and the versatility of players like **Marion Motley** and **Dante Lavelli**, made them virtually unstoppable.

The Browns' success in the AAFC was not a one-time phenomenon. They went on to win all four AAFC championships from 1946 to 1949, establishing themselves as one of the greatest teams in professional football history. Their dominance in the AAFC was so overwhelming that when the league merged with the NFL in 1950, many were skeptical about how the Browns would fare against the established NFL teams. However, the Browns quickly silenced their critics by winning the NFL Championship in their first season in the league.

The birth of the Cleveland Browns was a defining moment in professional football. Under Paul Brown's leadership, the team set a new standard for excellence and innovation, leaving an indelible mark on the sport. The Browns' early success not only solidified their place in football history but also influenced the evolution of the game, as many of Paul Brown's coaching methods became widely adopted across the league.

The 1946 Championship Game

The 1946 Championship Game marked a significant moment in the history of professional football, as it was the inaugural championship of the All-America Football Conference (AAFC). The game pitted the Cleveland Browns, who had dominated the regular season, against the New York Yankees, another strong contender in the league. This matchup was highly anticipated, as it was the culmination of a season that had seen the AAFC establish itself as a serious rival to the NFL.

The Cleveland Browns, under the leadership of **Paul Brown**, had quickly become the team to beat in the AAFC. They finished the regular season with an impressive 12-2 record, showcasing a potent offense led by quarterback **Otto Graham** and a formidable defense. The New York Yankees, coached by **Ray Flaherty**, were no slouches either, finishing the season with a 10-3-1 record. The Yankees were known for their balanced attack and strong defense, making them a worthy opponent for the Browns.

The championship game was held on December 22, 1946, at Cleveland Municipal Stadium, with over 40,000 fans in attendance. The weather was cold and windy, typical of a Cleveland winter, but the conditions did little to dampen the enthusiasm of the crowd. The game was expected to be a close contest, given the strength of both teams, but it quickly became clear that the Browns were the superior team on the day.

Cleveland took control early, with Otto Graham directing a series of efficient drives that resulted in points. The Browns' offense was a well-oiled machine, executing Paul Brown's game plan with precision. Graham connected with his favorite targets, **Dante Lavelli** and **Mac Speedie**, for key completions, while running back **Marion Motley** pounded the ball on the ground, wearing down the Yankees' defense.

On the defensive side, the Browns were equally dominant. They stifled the Yankees' offense, led by quarterback **Ace Parker**, and forced several turnovers. The Browns' defense, anchored by players like **Bill Willis** and **Walt Michaels**, played with discipline and intensity, allowing the Yankees little room to maneuver.

The final score was 14-9 in favor of the Browns, a victory that was more comfortable than the scoreline might suggest. The win capped off a remarkable season for Cleveland and affirmed their status as the premier team in the AAFC. For Paul Brown, it was a vindication of his coaching methods and a validation of the team he had meticulously assembled.

The 1946 Championship Game was more than just the first title for the Cleveland Browns; it was a statement that the AAFC was a legitimate and competitive league. The success of the Browns in this game and throughout the season demonstrated that professional football was entering a new era of sophistication and skill, one that would eventually lead to the merging of the AAFC and the NFL, and the further growth of the sport as a national pastime.

CHAPTER 6: THE 1950S - A DECADE OF CHANGE

The NFL-AFL Rivalry Begins

The rivalry between the NFL and the AFL began in the late 1950s and quickly became one of the most defining and transformative periods in the history of American football. This intense competition not only changed the landscape of professional football but also set the stage for the eventual merger that would create the modern NFL.

The seeds of the NFL-AFL rivalry were sown in 1959 when a group of businessmen, frustrated by their inability to secure NFL franchises, decided to form a new professional football league. Led by Lamar Hunt, the son of Texas oil magnate H.L. Hunt, these entrepreneurs believed there was room for more professional football teams in the United States. The NFL, by then a well-established league with significant media contracts and a loyal fan base, had turned away many potential owners, leaving them with few options but to start their own league.

Lamar Hunt's vision materialized in 1960 with the formation of the American Football League (AFL). The AFL started with eight teams, known as the "Foolish Club" because many doubted the league's chances of success. These teams included the **Dallas Texans** (later the Kansas City Chiefs), **Houston Oilers**, **Buffalo Bills**, and **New York Titans** (later the Jets). The AFL positioned itself as a direct competitor to the NFL, not just by existing but by challenging the older league on multiple fronts.

One of the first major battles in the NFL-AFL rivalry was over talent. The AFL aggressively pursued top college players, offering them lucrative contracts that often exceeded what the NFL was willing to pay. This competition for players drove up salaries and forced both leagues to invest more heavily in their rosters. The bidding wars became so intense that by the mid-1960s, some players were signing contracts with both leagues, leading to legal battles and public disputes.

The AFL also sought to differentiate itself with a more exciting and fan-friendly brand of football. The league emphasized the passing game more than the NFL, with wide-open offenses that appealed to fans who enjoyed high-scoring contests. The AFL's willingness to innovate extended to its television deals as well. The league secured a landmark contract with ABC, giving it a national television presence that rivaled the NFL's broadcasts. This exposure helped the AFL gain a foothold in the American sports landscape, as fans across the country became familiar with its teams and stars.

As the rivalry heated up, tensions between the two leagues grew. The NFL initially dismissed the AFL as a minor league, but the new league's success and the escalating competition for talent forced the NFL to take the threat seriously. The situation reached a boiling point in 1965 when Joe Namath, one of the most sought-after college quarterbacks, signed with the AFL's New York Jets for a record $427,000, a staggering sum at the time. Namath's decision to choose the AFL over the NFL sent shockwaves through the football world and underscored the AFL's growing influence.

The rivalry wasn't limited to player acquisitions. The two leagues also competed fiercely for fans, sponsorships, and media attention. The AFL's bold, brash style contrasted with the more conservative NFL, creating a dynamic that attracted a younger, more diverse audience. Cities that had been overlooked by the NFL, like Houston and Denver, found new sports heroes in the AFL, further deepening the rivalry.

By the mid-1960s, it became clear that the escalating costs of competition were unsustainable for both leagues. The NFL and AFL were spending vast amounts of money to outbid each other for players and market dominance. This financial strain led to discussions about a merger, which culminated in the historic agreement in 1966 to combine the two leagues. The merger was completed in 1970, forming a unified National Football League with two conferences: the NFC (composed of the original NFL teams) and the AFC (composed of the former AFL teams).

The NFL-AFL rivalry was a period of intense competition that ultimately benefited the sport of football. It led to higher salaries for players, more exciting football for fans, and the expansion of professional football into new markets. The rivalry also set the stage for the Super Bowl, which began as a championship game between the two leagues and has since become the most-watched sporting event in the United States. The rivalry's legacy is still felt today, as the NFL continues to build on the innovations and lessons learned during that transformative era.

The Rise of Television and Football

The rise of television in the 1950s and 1960s dramatically transformed professional football, turning the NFL into a national spectacle and bringing the sport into the homes of millions of Americans. Before television, football was primarily a regional pastime, with fans attending games in person or listening to radio broadcasts. However, as television became more accessible, it offered the NFL an unprecedented platform to reach a broader audience.

One of the first major steps in the NFL's relationship with television came in 1956 when the league signed a contract with CBS to televise its games nationwide. This agreement was a game-changer for the NFL, providing the league with a steady stream of revenue and exposing football to a national audience. The visual appeal of the sport, with its dynamic plays, intense action, and larger-than-life personalities, made it perfect for television. Fans who had never been able to attend a game in person could now watch their favorite teams and players from the comfort of their living rooms.

Television not only expanded the NFL's reach but also influenced the way the game was played and presented. Games were scheduled to fit into TV slots, leading to the standardization of start times and the introduction of instant replay to enhance the viewing experience. Coaches and players became more aware of the power of television, leading to more strategic, and sometimes dramatic, play calling that could captivate the viewing audience.

The NFL's embrace of television also led to the creation of iconic broadcasts, such as **Monday Night Football**, which debuted in 1970. This prime-time slot introduced a new level of spectacle to the game, combining sports with entertainment and attracting a diverse audience. The success of Monday Night Football demonstrated the immense drawing power of the NFL and solidified its status as America's favorite sport.

Television also had a big impact in building the NFL's brand and creating a national fan base. As fans became more familiar with teams and players from across the country, rivalries intensified, and the league's stars became household names. The ability to watch games from anywhere in the country helped to turn the NFL into a national obsession, with fans passionately following the action week after week.

The rise of television and football was a mutually beneficial relationship that transformed both the sport and the medium. For the NFL, television was the key to reaching new heights of popularity and financial success. For television networks, football became a reliable ratings juggernaut, drawing millions of viewers and generating significant advertising revenue. This symbiotic relationship continues to shape the NFL today, as the league remains one of the most-watched and commercially successful sports organizations in the world.

The Legendary 1958 NFL Championship Game

The 1958 NFL Championship Game, often referred to as "The Greatest Game Ever Played," holds a legendary place in football history. Played on December 28, 1958, at Yankee Stadium in New York City, this game between the Baltimore Colts and the New York Giants not only showcased the drama and excitement of professional football but also played a pivotal role in catapulting the NFL into the national spotlight.

The game featured two of the league's best teams: the Colts, led by the legendary quarterback **Johnny Unitas**, and the Giants, boasting a stout defense anchored by **Sam Huff** and a skilled offense led by quarterback **Charlie Conerly**. Both teams had strong seasons, setting the stage for a highly anticipated championship matchup.

The game itself was a back-and-forth battle, with neither team able to pull away decisively. The Giants took an early lead, but the Colts, known for their resilience and offensive firepower, kept the game close. Johnny Unitas, known for his cool demeanor and pinpoint passing, orchestrated several crucial drives that kept the Colts in contention.

As the clock wound down, the Giants held a 17-14 lead, and it seemed they might secure the championship. However, Unitas led a last-minute drive that culminated in a field goal by **Steve Myhra**, tying the game at 17-17 and sending it into sudden-death overtime—the first in NFL championship history. The introduction of sudden-death overtime added an extra layer of drama, as the first team to score would win the game.

In overtime, Unitas once again took control, methodically driving the Colts down the field with a series of precise passes and strategic runs. The drive ended with a 1-yard touchdown run by **Alan Ameche**, giving the Colts a 23-17 victory. The game's dramatic conclusion, with Unitas and the Colts prevailing in overtime, became an instant classic.

The 1958 Championship Game was broadcast live on national television, exposing millions of viewers to the excitement and intensity of professional football. The game's thrilling finish and the high level of play captivated the audience and left a lasting impression on the American public. It was a watershed moment for the NFL, demonstrating the sport's potential as a major entertainment spectacle.

This game not only solidified Johnny Unitas's legacy as one of the greatest quarterbacks of all time but also marked the beginning of the NFL's rise to prominence in American culture. The 1958 Championship Game is often credited with helping to establish the NFL as the most popular sport in the United States, setting the stage for the league's explosive growth in the following decades.

The Growth of NFL Popularity

The NFL's popularity grew rapidly in the 1950s and 1960s, transforming the league from a regional pastime into a national obsession. Several key factors contributed to this explosive growth, including the rise of television, the league's embrace of innovation, and the emergence of legendary players and teams that captured the public's imagination.

Television was perhaps the most significant driver of the NFL's increasing popularity. As TV sets became more common in American households, the NFL capitalized on the medium's ability to bring the game to a nationwide audience. The league's partnership with CBS, which began in 1956, was a game-changer. For the first time, fans across the country could watch their favorite teams and players in real-time, creating a shared national experience around the sport. Iconic broadcasts, such as **Monday Night Football**, further cemented the NFL's place in American culture, making football a central part of the weekly routine for millions of viewers.

The NFL's willingness to innovate also was important in its growth. The league introduced several changes that made the game more exciting and fan-friendly. The adoption of the **sudden-death overtime** rule, the creation of the **two-point conversion**, and the development of instant replay all contributed to a more dynamic and engaging sport. These innovations kept fans on the edge of their seats and made the NFL product more appealing to a broader audience.

The emergence of legendary players and teams during this era also helped to fuel the NFL's popularity. Stars like **Johnny Unitas**, **Bart Starr**, and **Jim Brown** became household names, not just for their on-field performances but also for their larger-than-life personas. These players, along with iconic teams like the **Green Bay Packers** under **Vince Lombardi**, drew fans in with their skill, determination, and winning ways. The Packers' dominance in the 1960s, culminating in victories in the first two Super Bowls, established them as one of the most storied franchises in NFL history and contributed to the league's growing allure.

Another factor in the NFL's rise was its ability to cultivate and promote rivalries. Games between teams like the Packers and the Chicago Bears, or the Dallas Cowboys and the New York Giants, became must-watch events that drew massive crowds and significant media attention. These rivalries, often rooted in regional pride and long histories, intensified fan engagement and loyalty, further boosting the league's popularity.

The NFL's growth during the 1950s and 1960s was also supported by the league's strong leadership. Commissioners like **Bert Bell** and **Pete Rozelle** understood the importance of marketing, media relations, and maintaining competitive balance within the league. Under their guidance, the NFL expanded its reach, increased its television presence, and ensured that every team had a chance to compete for championships, making the league more attractive to fans across the country.

By the end of the 1960s, the NFL had firmly established itself as America's favorite sport. The league's ability to innovate, promote its stars, and capitalize on the power of television transformed professional football into a cultural phenomenon, setting the stage for the NFL's continued dominance in the decades to come.

Key Players and Teams of the 1950s

The 1950s were a transformative decade for the NFL, marked by the emergence of iconic players and dominant teams that helped shape the future of professional football. This era produced some of the sport's greatest legends and laid the groundwork for the NFL's rise to prominence in American culture.

Johnny Unitas, the legendary quarterback for the Baltimore Colts, was one of the most influential players of the 1950s. Known for his poise, accuracy, and leadership, Unitas revolutionized the quarterback position. His ability to orchestrate game-winning drives, particularly in clutch situations, became a defining feature of his career. Unitas led the Colts to back-to-back NFL championships in 1958 and 1959, cementing his legacy as one of the greatest quarterbacks of all time. His performance in the 1958 NFL Championship Game, often referred to as "The Greatest Game Ever Played," is still celebrated as a defining moment in football history.

Another key figure of the 1950s was **Jim Brown**, the Cleveland Browns' powerhouse running back who redefined the role of a running back in professional football. Brown's combination of speed, power, and agility made him nearly unstoppable on the field. He led the league in rushing yards for eight of his nine seasons and was named the NFL's Most Valuable Player in 1957. Brown's dominance as a running back not only earned him a place in the Pro Football Hall of Fame but also changed how the position was perceived and utilized.

The **Cleveland Browns** were one of the standout teams of the 1950s, consistently performing at a high level under the leadership of head coach **Paul Brown**. The Browns won the NFL Championship in 1950, their first year in the league after the AAFC-NFL merger, and continued to be a dominant force throughout the decade. Paul Brown's innovative coaching techniques, including the use of playbooks, film study, and the development of the modern pass-blocking scheme, set new standards for the sport and influenced generations of coaches.

Another dominant team of the 1950s was the **Detroit Lions**, who won three NFL Championships in 1952, 1953, and 1957. Led by quarterback **Bobby Layne** and a formidable defense, the Lions were known for their gritty, hard-nosed style of play. Layne, a tough and charismatic leader, was instrumental in the Lions' success, earning a reputation as one of the best quarterbacks of his era.

The **New York Giants** also emerged as a powerhouse during the latter half of the decade, thanks to a defense anchored by linebacker **Sam Huff** and a strategic approach under head coach **Jim Lee Howell** and offensive coordinator **Vince Lombardi**. The Giants' innovative use of defensive schemes, including the zone blitz, made them one of the most feared teams in the league.

49

The 1950s were a decade of change and growth for the NFL, driven by the contributions of legendary players and the success of dominant teams. The impact of these players and teams not only defined the era but also set the stage for the NFL's continued evolution and popularity in the years to come.

The Rise of the Two-Platoon System

The rise of the two-platoon system in the 1950s marked a significant shift in how football was played, fundamentally changing the structure of the game and the roles of its players. Before the adoption of this system, football was played under what was known as the "one-platoon" or "ironman" system, where players were required to play both offense and defense. This approach demanded a high level of versatility from players but also limited the specialization that could be achieved in each phase of the game.

The shift towards the two-platoon system began during World War II when player shortages forced teams to adapt. Coaches started experimenting with separate units for offense and defense, allowing players to focus on mastering one side of the ball. This experimentation laid the groundwork for the post-war adoption of the system, which would soon become the standard in both college and professional football.

The two-platoon system was officially adopted in the NFL in the early 1950s, with teams like the **Cleveland Browns** and the **New York Giants** leading the way. The system allowed for greater specialization, as players could now dedicate themselves entirely to either offensive or defensive roles. This led to the development of more sophisticated strategies and the emergence of position-specific skills that elevated the overall quality of play.

On offense, the two-platoon system enabled the creation of more complex and dynamic playbooks. Quarterbacks could now work exclusively with their offensive units to refine timing, routes, and blocking schemes, leading to more efficient and explosive offenses. Players like **Johnny Unitas** and **Jim Brown** thrived in this environment, as they could focus on perfecting their craft without the fatigue of playing both sides of the ball.

Defensively, the two-platoon system allowed for the development of specialized roles such as pass rushers, cover corners, and run-stopping linebackers. Coaches like **Tom Landry**, who served as the defensive coordinator for the New York Giants, began to innovate with new defensive formations and strategies, such as the 4-3 defense, which became a cornerstone of modern football. The specialization also led to the emergence of defensive stars like **Sam Huff**, whose ability to read offenses and make quick adjustments became a model for future linebackers.

The rise of the two-platoon system also had a profound impact on the physical demands of the game. Players could now push themselves to the limits on every play, knowing they had a dedicated unit to take over when the possession changed. This increased intensity and pace made the game more exciting for fans and contributed to the NFL's growing popularity during the 1950s.

The adoption of the two-platoon system was a crucial development in the evolution of football, allowing for greater specialization, strategic depth, and overall improvement in the quality of play. It marked the beginning of modern football as we know it today, where specialization and strategy are key components of the game.

Strategic & Schematic Evolutions in the 1950s

The 1950s were a period of significant strategic and schematic evolution in the NFL, as coaches and players began to explore new ways to gain a competitive edge. These innovations laid the foundation for many of the modern strategies that are still used in football today, transforming the game from a straightforward, run-heavy contest into a complex and dynamic sport.

One of the most important developments of the 1950s was the refinement of the **T-formation** offense, which had been introduced in the 1940s but came into full bloom during this decade. The T-formation, which placed the quarterback directly under center with three running backs lined up behind him, allowed for greater versatility in play-calling. It enabled teams to execute a wider variety of running plays and introduced the concept of play-action passing, where the quarterback fakes a handoff to draw in the defense before passing the ball. This deception added a new layer of complexity to offensive play and made defending against the pass more challenging.

The **Cleveland Browns**, under head coach **Paul Brown**, were pioneers in advancing offensive strategy during this period. Paul Brown is credited with innovating the use of detailed playbooks and film study, which allowed his team to execute plays with precision and consistency. He also introduced the concept of the **pocket passer**—a quarterback who primarily operates from within the protective "pocket" formed by the offensive line. This approach maximized the quarterback's time to survey the field and make accurate throws, leading to the development of more sophisticated passing attacks.

Defensively, the 1950s saw the introduction of the **4-3 defense**, which became the standard formation for many NFL teams. The 4-3 defense, developed by coaches like **Tom Landry** of the New York Giants, positioned four defensive linemen and three linebackers on the field. This setup provided a strong front to stop the run while still allowing flexibility to defend against the pass. The 4-3 defense also enabled the introduction of specialized roles within the defensive unit, such as the pass-rushing defensive end and the coverage linebacker, which added depth and variety to defensive strategies.

Another significant strategic evolution during this decade was the increased use of **zone coverage** in the secondary. Instead of assigning each defender to a specific receiver, zone coverage had defenders guarding designated areas of the field. This approach was particularly effective against the growing trend of passing offenses, as it allowed defenses to better anticipate and react to passing plays, reducing the effectiveness of deep throws and quick slant routes.

The 1950s also witnessed the beginning of more **pre-snap adjustments**, where both offensive and defensive players would change their alignments or assignments based on the opponent's formation and tendencies. This increased the mental aspect of the game, as players had to be well-versed in both their own playbook and the likely strategies of their opponents.

These strategic and schematic evolutions during the 1950s was important in the development of modern football. The innovations introduced in this decade not only made the game more complex and exciting but also set the stage for the advanced strategies and high-level play that define the NFL today.

CHAPTER 7: THE AFL AND NFL MERGER (1960S)

The Formation of the AFL

The formation of the American Football League (AFL) in 1959 was a bold and transformative moment in the history of professional football. The AFL was born out of frustration and ambition, driven by a group of wealthy businessmen who were eager to bring professional football to cities that had been overlooked by the National Football League (NFL). Their vision for the AFL would not only challenge the dominance of the NFL but also set the stage for the eventual merger that would reshape the landscape of American sports.

The story of the AFL's formation begins with **Lamar Hunt**, a young and determined businessman from Texas. Hunt, the son of oil tycoon H.L. Hunt, had a passion for sports and a keen interest in football. In the late 1950s, Lamar Hunt attempted to secure an NFL franchise for his hometown of Dallas, but his efforts were repeatedly rebuffed by the NFL, which was not interested in expanding at the time. Frustrated but undeterred, Hunt began to explore the idea of starting a new professional football league.

Hunt quickly found like-minded individuals who shared his vision. Among them were **Bud Adams** of Houston, **Barron Hilton** of Los Angeles, and **Ralph Wilson** of Buffalo. Together, these men formed the core of what would become the AFL's ownership group, often referred to as the "Foolish Club" because of the skepticism surrounding their venture. Despite the doubts of many in the sports world, these owners were committed to creating a league that would compete directly with the NFL.

The AFL officially launched in 1960 with eight teams: the **Boston Patriots, Buffalo Bills, Dallas Texans, Denver Broncos, Houston Oilers, Los Angeles Chargers, New York Titans**, and **Oakland Raiders**. Each of these franchises was strategically located in markets that either lacked an NFL presence or had been underserved by professional football. The AFL's owners understood that for their league to succeed, they needed to establish a strong identity and attract fans who were eager for football in their cities.

One of the AFL's key strategies was to differentiate itself from the NFL by offering a more exciting and fan-friendly style of play. The league emphasized the passing game, with wide-open offenses that featured deep throws and high-scoring contests. This approach was in stark contrast to the more conservative, run-oriented style that dominated the NFL at the time. The AFL's emphasis on offense made it popular with fans who enjoyed fast-paced, high-energy football.

The AFL also made a significant impact in the area of player recruitment. The league aggressively pursued top college talent, often outbidding the NFL for star players. This strategy led to a series of bidding wars between the two leagues, driving up salaries and raising the profile of professional football. One of the AFL's biggest early successes was signing **Joe Namath**, a highly sought-after quarterback from the University of Alabama, to the New York Jets for a then-record $427,000. Namath's signing brought instant credibility to the AFL and underscored the league's determination to compete with the NFL.

Despite facing financial challenges in its early years, the AFL gradually gained traction with fans and began to establish itself as a legitimate rival to the NFL. The league's innovative approach, combined with its commitment to expanding professional football into new markets, helped to build a loyal fan base and attract television contracts that provided much-needed revenue.

The formation of the AFL was a pivotal moment in the history of professional football. It challenged the NFL's dominance, introduced new ideas and innovations to the game, and ultimately led to the historic AFL-NFL merger in 1970. The AFL's influence can still be felt today, as many of the league's innovations, such as its emphasis on the passing game and its commitment to expanding football's reach, have become integral parts of the modern NFL.

Early AFL-NFL Competition

The early competition between the American Football League (AFL) and the National Football League (NFL) in the 1960s was intense and transformative, reshaping the landscape of professional football in the United States. This rivalry, driven by both leagues' desire to assert dominance, led to a period of fierce competition for players, fans, and media attention, ultimately paving the way for the historic merger between the two leagues.

When the AFL was founded in 1960, the NFL had already been established for four decades and was the premier professional football league in the country. However, the AFL quickly positioned itself as a formidable competitor by targeting markets that the NFL had overlooked and by implementing innovative strategies to attract both players and fans. The AFL's commitment to a more exciting, pass-heavy style of play appealed to many football enthusiasts, and the league began to build a dedicated following.

One of the most significant aspects of the AFL-NFL competition was the battle for top college talent. The AFL aggressively pursued college stars, often outbidding the NFL for their services. This led to a series of high-profile bidding wars, most notably for players like **Joe Namath**, who signed with the AFL's New York Jets for a record $427,000. These bidding wars not only drove up player salaries but also brought national attention to the AFL, forcing the NFL to take the new league seriously.

The competition wasn't limited to player acquisitions. The AFL and NFL also vied for television contracts, which were crucial for the financial success and visibility of both leagues. The AFL secured a landmark deal with ABC, giving the league a national television presence that helped it gain credibility and attract a broader audience. This TV exposure allowed the AFL to showcase its exciting brand of football, further fueling the rivalry with the NFL.

As the competition between the two leagues intensified, tensions began to rise. The NFL, initially dismissive of the AFL, soon realized that the upstart league was a genuine threat to its dominance. The bidding wars for players were becoming increasingly costly, and the competition for fans and media coverage was eroding the profitability of both leagues. By the mid-1960s, it became clear that the fierce competition between the AFL and NFL was unsustainable in the long term.

The intense rivalry between the AFL and NFL in the early 1960s was a period of significant change in professional football. It not only pushed both leagues to innovate and improve but also set the stage for the eventual merger that would create the modern NFL. The early competition between the AFL and NFL was a driving force behind the evolution of the sport, leading to higher player salaries, increased media coverage, and ultimately, the creation of the Super Bowl, which would become the pinnacle of professional football.

Key Figures in the Merger

The merger between the AFL and NFL in the late 1960s was one of the most significant events in the history of professional football, and it was driven by a group of key figures whose vision and leadership were instrumental in bringing the two leagues together. These individuals recognized that the intense competition between the AFL and NFL was unsustainable and that a merger would benefit both leagues, ensuring the long-term success of professional football in the United States.

Pete Rozelle, the commissioner of the NFL at the time, was a key figure in the merger negotiations. Rozelle, who became commissioner in 1960, was a strong advocate for the unification of the two leagues. He understood that the ongoing bidding wars for players and the competition for television contracts were harming both leagues financially. Rozelle's diplomatic skills and ability to bring people together were essential in navigating the complex negotiations that eventually led to the merger agreement.

On the AFL side, **Lamar Hunt**, the founder of the league and owner of the Kansas City Chiefs, was a key figure in the merger discussions. Hunt had always envisioned the AFL as a league that could compete on equal footing with the NFL, but he also recognized that the escalating costs of competition were threatening the viability of both leagues. Hunt's willingness to engage in constructive dialogue with NFL owners and his commitment to finding a solution that would benefit all parties were crucial in moving the merger forward.

Tex Schramm, the general manager of the Dallas Cowboys, was another influential figure in the merger process. Schramm, known for his innovative thinking and strategic vision, was a strong advocate for the merger. He believed that a unified league would create a more stable and prosperous environment for professional football. Schramm's close relationship with Lamar Hunt and his ability to build consensus among NFL owners were instrumental in overcoming the obstacles that stood in the way of the merger.

Al Davis, the head coach and general manager of the Oakland Raiders and later the commissioner of the AFL, also played a significant role in the merger. Davis was a fierce competitor who had led the AFL's aggressive campaign to sign top NFL players, but he eventually recognized that the long-term survival of the AFL required cooperation with the NFL. Davis's participation in the merger talks, particularly after he became AFL commissioner, helped to ensure that the interests of both leagues were represented in the final agreement.

The merger between the AFL and NFL, which was finalized in 1966 and fully implemented in 1970, would not have been possible without the efforts of these key figures. Their vision, leadership, and willingness to work together were instrumental in creating the modern NFL, a unified league that has become one of the most successful and popular sports organizations in the world. The merger not only ended the rivalry between the two leagues but also set the stage for the growth and evolution of professional football in the decades that followed.

The Super Bowl is Born

The creation of the Super Bowl in the late 1960s was a direct result of the merger between the AFL and NFL, and it quickly became the most significant and celebrated event in American sports. The idea of a championship game between the two leagues had been discussed as early as 1966, but it wasn't until the merger agreement was finalized that the concept of the Super Bowl truly began to take shape.

The first Super Bowl, officially known as the AFL-NFL World Championship Game, was played on January 15, 1967, at the Los Angeles Memorial Coliseum. The game pitted the NFL champion **Green Bay Packers**, led by legendary coach **Vince**

Lombardi, against the AFL champion **Kansas City Chiefs**, owned by AFL founder **Lamar Hunt**. The game was the culmination of years of rivalry between the two leagues and was seen as a way to determine which league was truly superior.

Despite the hype surrounding the game, the first Super Bowl did not sell out, and the television ratings were lower than expected. However, the game itself was a success, with the Packers defeating the Chiefs 35-10 in a dominant performance that solidified the NFL's reputation as the stronger league. The Packers' victory, and their subsequent win in Super Bowl II, reinforced the idea that the NFL was the more established and competitive league, but the AFL's competitiveness would soon come to the forefront.

Super Bowl III, played on January 12, 1969, was the game that truly elevated the Super Bowl to its iconic status. The New York Jets, led by quarterback **Joe Namath**, faced the heavily favored Baltimore Colts. In the days leading up to the game, Namath famously guaranteed a Jets victory, a bold statement that captured the public's imagination. When the Jets defeated the Colts 16-7, it was seen as a monumental upset and a validation of the AFL's legitimacy. Namath's performance and the Jets' victory were defining moments in football history, proving that the AFL could compete with the best teams in the NFL.

The success of Super Bowl III helped to solidify the Super Bowl as the pinnacle of professional football. The game quickly grew in popularity, with each subsequent Super Bowl drawing larger audiences and generating more media attention. The Super Bowl became more than just a football game; it became a cultural phenomenon, with elaborate halftime shows, high-profile commercials, and a level of media coverage unmatched by any other sporting event.

The birth of the Super Bowl was a turning point for professional football. It provided a stage for the best teams from the AFL and NFL to compete, and it was important in unifying the two leagues into what would become the modern NFL. Today, the Super Bowl is the most-watched sporting event in the United States, one of the most-watched globally (only typically coming in behind the Champions League final and other major soccer matches – e.g., World Cup games), and is celebrated around the world, a testament to the enduring appeal of the game and the vision of those who helped to create it.

The Significance of the Merger for American Football

The merger between the American Football League (AFL) and the National Football League (NFL) in the late 1960s was a watershed moment in the history of American sports. It fundamentally altered the landscape of professional football, leading to the creation of the modern NFL, which would become the most popular and commercially successful sports league in the United States.

Before the merger, the AFL and NFL were engaged in a fierce rivalry. Both leagues competed intensely for players, fans, and media attention, leading to escalating costs and growing tension. The AFL, founded in 1960, had quickly established itself as a viable competitor to the NFL by introducing an exciting, pass-heavy style of play and aggressively recruiting top college talent. However, the financial strain of this competition was becoming increasingly unsustainable for both leagues.

The merger, finalized in 1966 and fully implemented in 1970, was significant for several reasons. First and foremost, it ended the costly bidding wars for players that had threatened the financial stability of both leagues. By unifying under a single entity, the NFL was able to create a more stable and profitable environment for professional football. The merged league adopted a common draft, which ensured that talent was distributed more evenly among teams, promoting competitive balance.

Another major significance of the merger was the expansion of the NFL's geographic and demographic reach. The AFL brought teams from cities that had previously been without professional football, including Kansas City, Denver, and Miami. This expansion helped to grow the NFL's fan base, making the league a truly national organization. The merger also introduced new styles of play and innovation, as AFL teams brought their high-scoring, offensive-minded approach to the NFL. This fusion of styles made the game more dynamic and exciting for fans.

The merger also had a profound impact on the media landscape. The creation of the Super Bowl as a championship game between the AFL and NFL champions became a cultural phenomenon. The Super Bowl quickly grew in popularity, becoming the most-watched sporting event in the United States. The success of the Super Bowl, coupled with the unified league's growing appeal, helped the NFL secure lucrative television contracts that fueled its rapid growth in the 1970s and beyond.

The merger also paved the way for the NFL to establish itself as a major player in the American sports industry. With the combined resources of the two leagues, the NFL was able to invest in marketing, stadium development, and player salaries, further elevating the league's profile and appeal. The merger also led to the development of modern revenue-sharing models, ensuring that all teams could benefit from the league's success and helping to maintain competitive balance.

In summary, the merger between the AFL and NFL was a pivotal event that transformed professional football in the United States. It ended a costly rivalry, expanded the league's reach, and laid the foundation for the NFL's future success. The merger not only unified the sport but also set the stage for the NFL to become the dominant force in American sports that it is today.

Strategic & Schematic Evolutions in the 1960s

The 1960s were a decade of significant strategic and schematic evolution in professional football, as coaches and players sought new ways to gain a competitive edge. This period saw the introduction of innovative tactics and formations that would become foundational elements of modern football. The merger of the AFL and NFL further accelerated these developments, as teams from both leagues brought their unique approaches to the game.

One of the most important strategic evolutions of the 1960s was the increased emphasis on the passing game. While the forward pass had been a part of football since the early 20th century, it was in the 1960s that it became a central element of offensive strategy. AFL teams, in particular, were known for their wide-open, high-scoring offenses that relied heavily on the passing game. Coaches like **Sid Gillman** of the San Diego Chargers pioneered the use of sophisticated passing schemes, including the deep passing attack and the use of multiple receiver formations. Gillman's offense spread the field horizontally and vertically, forcing defenses to cover more ground and creating opportunities for big plays.

The 1960s also saw the refinement of the **zone defense**, which became an essential tool for defending against the increasingly potent passing attacks. In a zone defense, defenders are responsible for covering specific areas of the field rather than individual receivers. This approach allowed defenses to better anticipate and react to passing plays, reducing the effectiveness of deep throws and quick slant routes. Coaches like **Tom Landry** of the Dallas Cowboys were instrumental in popularizing the zone defense, which became a staple of NFL defenses in the following decades.

Another significant schematic evolution of the 1960s was the development of the **4-3 defense**. While the 4-3 defense had been introduced in the 1950s, it was during the 1960s that it became the dominant defensive formation in the NFL. The 4-3 defense features four defensive linemen and three linebackers, providing a strong front against the run while maintaining flexibility to defend against the pass. This formation allowed for greater specialization within the defensive unit, with specific players assigned to rush the passer, stop the run, or cover receivers.

The 1960s also saw the rise of the **West Coast offense**, although it would not be named as such until the 1980s. This offensive approach, developed by **Bill Walsh** and others, emphasized short, quick passes as a substitute for the running game. The West Coast offense relied on precision timing and route running, with the quarterback delivering the ball quickly to receivers who could gain yards after the catch. This strategy minimized the risk of turnovers and allowed offenses to control the tempo of the game.

Special teams also became a more significant focus during the 1960s. Coaches began to place greater emphasis on the kicking game, recognizing the impact that field position and kick returns could have on the outcome of games. The introduction of specialized kickers and returners added a new dimension to the game, making special teams an integral part of football strategy.

The strategic and schematic evolutions of the 1960s laid the groundwork for many of the innovations that define modern football. The increased emphasis on the passing game, the development of new defensive strategies, and the refinement of offensive schemes all contributed to the evolution of the sport, making it more complex, dynamic, and exciting for players and fans alike. The innovations of this decade continue to influence the way football is played and coached today.

CHAPTER 8: THE SUPER BOWL ERA BEGINS (1970S)

The Emergence of the Super Bowl as a National Event

The 1970s marked the emergence of the Super Bowl as a defining national event, transforming from a mere championship game into the biggest spectacle in American sports. What began as a clash between the AFL and NFL champions quickly evolved into a cultural phenomenon that captured the attention of millions across the United States.

The early Super Bowls were significant, but it wasn't until Super Bowl III in 1969 that the game truly began to gain national prominence. **Joe Namath's** famous guarantee of victory and the subsequent upset by the New York Jets over the heavily favored Baltimore Colts shocked the sports world. This moment put the Super Bowl on the map as a must-watch event, signaling the AFL's legitimacy and raising the stakes for future championships.

As the NFL fully absorbed the AFL following the 1970 merger, the Super Bowl became the culminating event of the new, unified league. The game's significance grew with each passing year, fueled by the dominance of iconic teams like the **Pittsburgh Steelers**, who won four Super Bowls in the 1970s, and the **Dallas Cowboys**, whose "America's Team" moniker reflected their broad national appeal. These teams brought star power and compelling storylines, which drew in casual fans and solidified the Super Bowl's place in American culture.

Television was vital in the Super Bowl's rise. The advent of color TV and the expanding reach of broadcast networks brought the game into millions of homes. By the mid 1970s, the Super Bowl was consistently the most-watched program in the United States, attracting audiences far beyond the typical football fan base. The spectacle of the game was amplified by elaborate halftime shows and the growing tradition of high-profile commercials, which became an integral part of the viewing experience. The Super Bowl became as much about entertainment and advertising as it was about the football game itself.

The NFL's marketing strategy also contributed to the Super Bowl's growing importance. The league promoted the game as the ultimate test of skill, strategy, and perseverance, tapping into the American values of competition and excellence. The Super Bowl's branding as "the big game" resonated with audiences, making it an annual event where families and friends gathered to watch, regardless of their usual interest in football.

By the end of the 1970s, the Super Bowl had firmly established itself as a national event, an occasion that transcended sports to become a part of American culture.

The game's ability to bring people together, create memorable moments, and set records for television viewership underscored its significance. The emergence of the Super Bowl as a national event in the 1970s set the stage for it to become the global phenomenon it is today, where the game, the commercials, and the halftime show all contribute to its status as the biggest event in American sports.

Dominant Teams of the 1970s

The 1970s were a golden era in NFL history, dominated by a few powerhouse teams that left an indelible mark on the league. These teams not only won championships but also defined the style of play and set the standard for excellence that others aspired to match.

At the forefront of this dominance were the **Pittsburgh Steelers**, who emerged as the team of the decade. The Steelers, under head coach **Chuck Noll**, built a dynasty that won four Super Bowls in six years (1974, 1975, 1978, 1979). The foundation of their success was the **"Steel Curtain"** defense, a formidable unit led by legends like **Joe Greene**, **Jack Lambert**, **Jack Ham**, and **Mel Blount**. This defense was virtually impenetrable, combining physical toughness with a strategic mastery that stifled opposing offenses. On the offensive side, the Steelers were anchored by quarterback **Terry Bradshaw** and wide receivers **Lynn Swann** and **John Stallworth**, whose big plays became a hallmark of Pittsburgh's success. The Steelers' ability to dominate on both sides of the ball made them the defining team of the 1970s.

Another dominant team of the 1970s was the **Dallas Cowboys**, often referred to as "America's Team." Under the leadership of head coach **Tom Landry**, the Cowboys were known for their innovative offense, the **flex defense**, and a roster filled with star talent. The Cowboys appeared in five Super Bowls during the decade, winning two (1971 and 1977). Quarterback **Roger Staubach** became the face of the franchise, known for his leadership and clutch performances. The Cowboys were also known for their meticulous preparation and strategic approach, which allowed them to consistently compete at the highest level. Players like **Tony Dorsett**, **Drew Pearson**, and **Randy White** helped solidify the Cowboys' reputation as a perennial contender throughout the 1970s.

The **Miami Dolphins** were another team that left a significant mark on the 1970s, particularly with their historic 1972 season. Under head coach **Don Shula**, the Dolphins achieved the only perfect season in NFL history, finishing 17-0 and winning Super Bowl VII. The Dolphins followed up with another Super Bowl victory in 1973, cementing their place among the elite teams of the decade. The Dolphins' success was built on a balanced offense led by quarterback **Bob Griese** and running backs **Larry Csonka** and **Mercury Morris**, as well as a strong defense known as the **"No-Name Defense."** Their ability to dominate both the regular season and the postseason made the Dolphins one of the most respected teams of the 1970s.

These teams—the Steelers, Cowboys, and Dolphins—defined the 1970s in the NFL. Their success on the field, combined with their iconic players and innovative strategies, not only brought them championships but also left a lasting legacy that continues to influence the NFL today.

Key Players of the Decade

The 1970s were a decade that saw the emergence of some of the most iconic players in NFL history. These athletes not only excelled on the field but also became symbols of the toughness, skill, and charisma that defined football during this era.

One of the most significant players of the 1970s was **Terry Bradshaw**, the quarterback of the Pittsburgh Steelers. Bradshaw's leadership and ability to perform under pressure were crucial to the Steelers' four Super Bowl victories during the decade. Known for his powerful arm and fearless playing style, Bradshaw was the MVP of Super Bowls XIII and XIV. His deep connection with wide receivers **Lynn Swann** and **John Stallworth** became one of the most potent offensive combinations in the NFL, and his contributions to the Steelers' dynasty earned him a place in the Pro Football Hall of Fame.

Another key player of the decade was **Roger Staubach**, the quarterback for the Dallas Cowboys. Staubach, nicknamed "Captain America," was known for his leadership, mobility, and ability to execute in clutch situations. He led the Cowboys to two Super Bowl victories (VI and XII) and was named Super Bowl MVP in 1972. Staubach's ability to make big plays, both with his arm and his legs, made him one of the most exciting players of the 1970s. His poise under pressure and his clean-cut image made him a beloved figure both on and off the field.

On the defensive side, **"Mean" Joe Greene** of the Pittsburgh Steelers was a dominant force. Greene was the anchor of the "Steel Curtain" defense, known for his fierce play and leadership. His ability to disrupt opposing offenses from the defensive tackle position was unmatched, and he was a key reason for the Steelers' success throughout the decade. Greene's intensity and impact on the field earned him multiple Defensive Player of the Year awards and solidified his legacy as one of the greatest defensive players in NFL history.

Running back **Walter Payton** of the Chicago Bears also emerged as a superstar in the 1970s. Known for his incredible work ethic and versatility, Payton was a relentless runner who could break tackles, catch passes, and block with equal proficiency. Payton's durability and consistent production made him the NFL's all-time leading rusher by the time of his retirement. His nickname, "Sweetness," belied his toughness on the field and his graceful running style.

Finally, **O.J. Simpson** of the Buffalo Bills was another key player of the 1970s. Simpson became the first player in NFL history to rush for over 2,000 yards in a single season (1973), a record that stood for many years. His explosive speed and ability to make defenders miss made him one of the most electrifying players of his time.

These players—Bradshaw, Staubach, Greene, Payton, and Simpson—were among the brightest stars of the 1970s. Their performances on the field and their influence on the game helped shape the NFL into the dynamic, competitive league that it is today.

NFL Rule Changes and Their Impact

The 1970s were a decade of significant rule changes in the NFL, many of which were designed to make the game safer, more exciting, and more balanced between offense and defense. These changes had a profound impact on how the game was played and contributed to the evolution of modern football.

One of the most impactful rule changes of the 1970s was the **introduction of the 1978 "Mel Blount Rule,"** named after the Pittsburgh Steelers' Hall of Fame cornerback. This rule restricted defensive players from making contact with receivers beyond five yards from the line of scrimmage. Before this rule, defenders like Blount could physically engage receivers throughout their routes, making it difficult for offenses to execute passing plays. The implementation of this rule opened up the passing game, leading to an increase in offensive production and helping to usher in the era of high-scoring games that became popular in the 1980s.

Another significant rule change was the **elimination of the head slap** for defensive linemen. Previously, defensive linemen were allowed to slap offensive linemen on the side of the helmet to gain an advantage. This technique was highly effective but also dangerous, leading to a high risk of concussions and other head injuries. The NFL banned the head slap in 1977 as part of a broader effort to improve player safety. This change forced defensive linemen to rely more on technique and strength rather than sheer aggression, altering the dynamics of line play.

The 1970s also saw changes to **kickoff rules**, aimed at reducing injuries and encouraging more exciting returns. The NFL moved the kickoff line from the 40-yard line to the 35-yard line in 1974, making it more difficult for kickers to reach the end zone and increasing the likelihood of kick returns. This rule change added an element of unpredictability to the game and made special teams play more significant, as teams now had greater opportunities to gain favorable field position through returns.

The **goalpost** location was another important change in the 1970s. In 1974, the NFL moved the goalposts from the goal line to the back of the end zone. This change reduced the number of field goals attempted and made it more challenging for kickers to score from long distances. The move was intended to reduce the reliance on field goals and encourage teams to attempt more touchdowns, making the game more exciting for fans.

Finally, the **introduction of overtime** in regular-season games in 1974 was a significant change that aimed to reduce the number of ties. The sudden-death format, where the first team to score in overtime wins, was implemented to ensure that games had a decisive outcome, adding drama and excitement to the regular season.

These rule changes in the 1970s had a lasting impact on the NFL, shaping the way the game is played today. By opening up the passing game, improving player safety, and making special teams more dynamic, these changes helped to modernize football and enhance its appeal to fans, contributing to the league's continued growth and success.

The Rise of Monday Night Football

The introduction of **Monday Night Football** in 1970 was a transformative moment in NFL history, fundamentally altering how football was presented and consumed by the American public. The concept of playing a prime-time game on Monday night was groundbreaking, providing the NFL with an unprecedented platform to showcase its product to a national audience.

The idea for Monday Night Football was spearheaded by **Roone Arledge**, the innovative head of sports programming at ABC. Arledge recognized the potential of football as a prime-time entertainment spectacle and worked closely with NFL Commissioner **Pete Rozelle** to bring the concept to life. Their collaboration led to the first Monday Night Football broadcast on September 21, 1970, featuring the New York Jets against the Cleveland Browns. The game was a success, drawing a large television audience and setting the stage for what would become a weekly tradition.

What set Monday Night Football apart was its production style, which was unlike anything seen in sports broadcasting at the time. Arledge and his team introduced multiple camera angles, instant replays, and a dynamic presentation that emphasized the drama and excitement of the game. The broadcast also featured a three-man announcing team, including **Howard Cosell, Don Meredith**, and **Keith Jackson** (later replaced by **Frank Gifford**). Cosell's outspoken and often controversial commentary, combined with Meredith's folksy charm, created a unique dynamic that captivated viewers and added an extra layer of entertainment to the games.

Monday Night Football quickly became more than just a football game; it became a cultural event. The prime-time slot allowed families and friends to gather and watch together, making it a shared experience that transcended the sport. The show's popularity grew rapidly, and by the mid-1970s, it was one of the highest-rated programs on television. The success of Monday Night Football demonstrated the immense drawing power of the NFL and solidified football's place as America's favorite sport.

The impact of Monday Night Football extended beyond television ratings. It helped to elevate the profile of the NFL and its players, turning them into household names. The exposure provided by Monday Night Football also attracted new fans to the sport, expanding the NFL's audience and helping to drive the league's growth throughout the 1970s and beyond.

Monday Night Football's influence on sports broadcasting cannot be overstated. It set the standard for how live sports were presented on television and inspired other leagues to seek prime-time exposure for their events. The show's success also paved the way for the NFL to secure lucrative television contracts, which would become a major source of revenue for the league.

The Impact of the NFL Players Association

The 1970s were a pivotal decade for the NFL Players Association (NFLPA), as the organization became a powerful advocate for players' rights, leading to significant changes in how the league operated. The NFLPA's efforts during this period laid the groundwork for many of the labor practices and protections that are still in place today.

Founded in 1956, the NFLPA initially struggled to gain traction in negotiations with the league's owners, who were resistant to the idea of a players' union. However, by the 1970s, the NFLPA had gained momentum, fueled by the growing awareness among players of the need for better wages, benefits, and working conditions. The organization's influence was bolstered by the appointment of **Ed Garvey** as its executive director in 1971. Garvey was a determined and savvy leader who understood the power of collective bargaining and was committed to improving the lives of NFL players.

One of the most significant achievements of the NFLPA in the 1970s was the negotiation of the first **collective bargaining agreement** (CBA) in NFL history, which was finalized in 1977. This agreement marked a major victory for the players, as it established important precedents for labor relations in the league. The CBA included provisions for improved player salaries, benefits, and working conditions. It also introduced the concept of **free agency**, albeit in a limited form, giving players more leverage in contract negotiations.

The NFLPA's advocacy also led to significant improvements in **health and safety standards** for players. The union pushed for better medical care, including the establishment of a pension plan and disability benefits for retired players. The NFLPA also fought for the implementation of safety measures to reduce the risk of injuries, such as stricter guidelines on player equipment and the introduction of new rules to protect players on the field.

The NFLPA's growing influence was not without resistance. The league's owners were often reluctant to concede to the union's demands, leading to several contentious labor disputes throughout the decade. The most notable of these was the **1974 players' strike**, the first in NFL history. Although the strike ultimately failed to achieve its immediate goals, it demonstrated the players' willingness to stand up for their rights and set the stage for future labor negotiations.

The impact of the NFLPA in the 1970s extended beyond the specific gains made in collective bargaining. The organization helped to shift the balance of power in the NFL, giving players a stronger voice in decisions that affected their careers and lives. The NFLPA's efforts during this decade also laid the foundation for the more equitable labor practices that would emerge in the following decades.

The NFLPA's work in the 1970s was crucial in transforming the relationship between players and owners, leading to a more professional and regulated environment in the NFL. The advancements in player rights and benefits achieved during this period continue to influence the league today, ensuring that players are treated with the respect and fairness they deserve.

Strategic & Schematic Evolutions in the 1970s

The 1970s were a decade of significant strategic and schematic evolution in the NFL, as coaches and teams sought to adapt to changes in the game and gain a competitive edge. This period saw the development of new offensive and defensive strategies that would shape the future of football and set the stage for the modern era.

One of the most notable strategic evolutions of the 1970s was the **expansion of the passing game**. The NFL had traditionally been a run-heavy league, but the introduction of rules that favored the passing game, such as the 1978 "Mel Blount Rule," which limited defensive contact with receivers, opened up new opportunities for offensive innovation. Coaches like **Don Coryell** of the San Diego Chargers pioneered the use of sophisticated passing schemes that spread the field and utilized multiple receivers. Coryell's offense, known as "Air Coryell," emphasized deep passes and vertical routes, revolutionizing the way teams approached the passing game and leading to an increase in offensive production across the league.

The 1970s also continued to see the rise of what would soon become known as the **West Coast offense**, a system developed by **Bill Walsh** that emphasized short, quick passes as a substitute for the running game. The West Coast offense relied on precise timing and route running, with the quarterback delivering the ball quickly to receivers who could gain yards after the catch. This strategy minimized the risk of turnovers and allowed offenses to control the tempo of the game. Walsh's innovative approach would become the foundation for many successful NFL offenses in the decades that followed.

On the defensive side, the 1970s were marked by the **evolution of zone defenses**, particularly the **Cover 2** and **Cover 3** schemes. These zone defenses were designed to counter the increasingly potent passing attacks by dividing the field into zones and assigning defenders to cover specific areas rather than individual receivers. The Cover 2 defense, popularized by teams like the Pittsburgh Steelers and the Dallas Cowboys, provided strong coverage against deep passes while still allowing defenders to stop the run. The use of zone defenses added a new layer of complexity to defensive strategy and made it more difficult for quarterbacks to find open receivers.

Another significant defensive innovation of the 1970s was the **introduction of the 3-4 defense**, which features three defensive linemen and four linebackers. This formation, pioneered by teams like the New England Patriots and the Miami Dolphins, provided greater flexibility in pass rushing and coverage. The 3-4 defense allowed teams to disguise their blitzes and create confusion for opposing quarterbacks, making it a highly effective strategy against the increasingly pass-oriented offenses of the 1970s.

Special teams also became more strategically important during the 1970s. Coaches began to place greater emphasis on field position, recognizing the impact that kickoffs, punts, and returns could have on the outcome of games. The introduction of specialized roles, such as the kickoff returner and the punter, added a new dimension to the game and made special teams an integral part of football strategy.

The strategic and schematic evolutions of the 1970s were driven by a desire to adapt to the changing dynamics of the game. Coaches and teams that embraced these innovations found success on the field, and many of the strategies developed during this decade continue to influence the way football is played today. The 1970s were a period of experimentation and growth that helped to shape the modern NFL and set the stage for the high-scoring, fast-paced game that fans enjoy today.

CHAPTER 9: THE 1980S - EXPANSION AND SCANDAL

The NFL Expands to New Markets

The 1980s were a pivotal decade for the NFL, marked by significant expansion into new markets as the league sought to solidify its position as America's premier sports organization. This period of growth was driven by the league's desire to reach untapped audiences and capitalize on the growing popularity of professional football across the country.

One of the most significant expansions occurred in 1982 when the NFL introduced the **San Diego Chargers** to the AFC West, filling a void in the Southern California market after the Oakland Raiders moved to Los Angeles. The Chargers brought a new fan base into the NFL fold, furthering the league's reach in a key region. San Diego's warm weather and large media market made it an attractive destination for the NFL, and the team quickly became an integral part of the league.

Another major expansion in the 1980s was the **Seattle Seahawks**, who joined the league in 1976 but truly found their footing in the 1980s. The Seahawks helped the NFL establish a presence in the Pacific Northwest, a region previously underserved by professional sports. Seattle's passionate fan base, known as the "12th Man," became legendary for its support, helping to make the Seahawks one of the most popular teams in the league.

The 1980s also saw the NFL expanding into the Southeastern United States with the establishment of the **Tampa Bay Buccaneers** in 1976. While the team struggled in its early years, it eventually found success, building a dedicated fan base in Florida. The Buccaneers' presence in Tampa Bay, along with the Miami Dolphins' established fan base, helped the NFL cement its popularity in the Southeast.

In 1984, the league took a bold step by approving the relocation of the **Baltimore Colts** to Indianapolis, marking one of the most controversial moves in NFL history. The Colts' relocation was driven by financial challenges in Baltimore and the promise of a new stadium in Indianapolis. Despite initial backlash, the move proved successful as the Colts thrived in their new home, attracting a strong fan base in the Midwest.

The NFL's expansion into new markets during the 1980s was not without its challenges, but it ultimately paid off, as the league solidified its presence in key regions across the United States. The addition of new teams and the relocation of existing franchises helped to create a more geographically diverse league, bringing professional football to millions of new fans.

This era of expansion laid the groundwork for the NFL's continued growth in the 1990s and beyond, as the league continued to explore new opportunities to reach untapped markets. The NFL's ability to adapt and expand during the 1980s was a testament to its leadership's vision and the sport's enduring appeal across the country.

The Influence of the West Coast Offense & 49ers Dominance

The West Coast Offense, developed by **Bill Walsh**, became one of the most influential strategic innovations in NFL history, and it was the foundation of the San Francisco 49ers' dominance throughout the 1980s. Walsh's system redefined how offenses operated, emphasizing precision, timing, and the short passing game to control the flow of the game and keep defenses off balance.

Bill Walsh, who became the head coach of the 49ers in 1979, introduced the West Coast Offense as a response to the traditional, run-heavy offenses that dominated the NFL at the time. Instead of relying on deep passes and a strong running game, Walsh's system focused on short, quick passes to receivers and running backs, allowing the offense to maintain a rhythm and move the ball methodically down the field. This approach was revolutionary, as it prioritized ball control and high-percentage passes, reducing the risk of turnovers and enabling the offense to dictate the pace of the game.

Central to the success of the West Coast Offense was the quarterback play of **Joe Montana**, who thrived under Walsh's system. Montana's accuracy, decision-making, and calm demeanor made him the perfect fit for Walsh's offense. His ability to quickly read defenses and deliver precise passes turned the 49ers' short passing game into a deadly weapon. Montana's connection with receivers like **Jerry Rice** and **Dwight Clark** became the hallmark of the 49ers' offense, leading to numerous big plays and game-winning drives.

The West Coast Offense also made extensive use of running backs in the passing game, utilizing players like **Roger Craig**, who became the first player in NFL history to gain 1,000 yards rushing and 1,000 yards receiving in a single season (1985). Craig's versatility exemplified the multifaceted nature of Walsh's offense, where every player had to be adept at both running and catching the ball.

The success of the West Coast Offense translated into dominance on the field. The 49ers won four Super Bowl titles in the 1980s (Super Bowls XVI, XIX, XXIII, and XXIV), establishing themselves as the team of the decade. Bill Walsh's innovative approach not only led to victories but also changed the way football was played.

Many teams across the NFL began to adopt elements of the West Coast Offense, recognizing its effectiveness in both short-yardage situations and sustaining long drives.

The influence of the West Coast Offense extended beyond the 1980s, as many of its principles are still used in modern NFL offenses. Bill Walsh's legacy, built on the success of the 49ers, continues to shape how football is coached and played, making the West Coast Offense one of the most enduring innovations in the history of the sport.

The USFL Challenge and Collapse

The United States Football League (USFL), founded in 1982, posed a significant challenge to the NFL during its brief existence. The USFL sought to capitalize on America's growing appetite for football by positioning itself as a legitimate alternative to the NFL, playing games in the spring and summer to avoid direct competition. While the league showed promise with innovative ideas and top-tier talent, it ultimately collapsed under financial strain and strategic missteps.

The USFL's strategy was to compete directly with the NFL by offering higher salaries and aggressively pursuing top college talent. The league succeeded in signing several high-profile players, including **Herschel Walker**, the 1982 Heisman Trophy winner, who became the face of the league when he joined the New Jersey Generals. The USFL also lured away NFL stars like **Steve Young** and **Reggie White**, adding credibility to its ambitions of becoming a major player in professional football.

In addition to attracting top talent, the USFL implemented innovative ideas that influenced the future of football. The league experimented with rules such as the two point conversion, which the NFL eventually adopted. The USFL also embraced a more open, pass-heavy style of play, which helped to make its games exciting and competitive. The league's willingness to innovate and take risks was a key part of its appeal to fans who were looking for something different from the traditional NFL model.

Despite its early success, the USFL's fortunes began to decline due to financial difficulties and internal disagreements. The decision to move the league's schedule to the fall, directly competing with the NFL, proved to be a critical mistake. This move, driven by the ambitious owners who believed they could force a merger with the NFL, backfired spectacularly. The USFL lacked the financial stability and television contracts needed to sustain such competition, leading to dwindling revenues and increased pressure on the league's resources.

The final blow came in the form of an antitrust lawsuit against the NFL, which the USFL won but was awarded only $1 in damages. The legal victory did nothing to alleviate the league's financial problems, and the USFL was forced to suspend operations before the 1986 season, effectively ending its existence.

The collapse of the USFL highlighted the challenges of competing with the NFL, which had established itself as the dominant force in American sports. While the USFL's failure was a setback for its investors and fans, the league's impact on football was lasting. Many of the players and ideas introduced by the USFL found their way into the NFL, influencing the game for years to come. The USFL's challenge to the NFL, though ultimately unsuccessful, remains a fascinating chapter in the history of professional football.

The NFL Players Strike of 1982

The NFL Players Strike of 1982 was a pivotal moment in the league's history, marking the first time that players walked out during the regular season. The strike, which lasted 57 days, began on September 21, 1982, and was driven by the players' demands for a better share of the league's revenue, particularly through improved salaries and benefits. At the heart of the dispute was the players' desire to secure a guaranteed percentage of the league's gross revenue, a concept that was new and controversial at the time.

The strike resulted in the cancellation of seven weeks of games, reducing the regular season from 16 to 9 games. This disruption led to considerable tension between the players, owners, and fans, who were frustrated by the prolonged labor dispute. Despite the challenges, the strike ultimately resulted in a new collective bargaining agreement that included the first revenue-sharing system in professional football, known as the "Rozelle Rule." This agreement also established the foundation for free agency, setting the stage for significant changes in the player-owner relationship in the years to come.

The 1982 strike underscored the growing power and influence of the NFL Players Association and highlighted the players' determination to secure fair compensation and working conditions. While the strike caused significant short-term disruption, its long-term impact was profound, reshaping the financial landscape of the NFL and empowering players in their negotiations with owners.

Strategic & Schematic Evolutions in the 1980s

The 1980s were a decade of strategic innovation and evolution in the NFL, as teams and coaches sought new ways to gain a competitive edge. While the West Coast Offense, developed by Bill Walsh, was one of the most influential innovations of the time, several other strategic developments also had a major role in shaping the modern game.

One of the most significant evolutions in the 1980s was the **increased use of the shotgun formation**. Originally introduced in the 1960s, the shotgun formation became more prevalent in the 1980s as teams recognized its value in passing situations. By placing the quarterback several yards behind the line of scrimmage, the shotgun provided more time to read defenses and avoid the pass rush. This formation became especially useful in third-down situations, where quick, accurate passing was essential. Coaches like **Tom Landry** of the Dallas Cowboys and **Don Coryell** of the San Diego Chargers were instrumental in popularizing the shotgun, using it to create more dynamic and unpredictable offenses.

Another key strategic development was the **emergence of the 3-4 defense** as a dominant defensive scheme. The 3-4 defense, featuring three defensive linemen and four linebackers, offered greater flexibility in pass rushing and coverage. This alignment allowed defenses to disguise their intentions more effectively, making it harder for quarterbacks to anticipate blitzes. Teams like the New York Giants, under defensive coordinator **Bill Belichick**, used the 3-4 defense to great effect, with players like **Lawrence Taylor** revolutionizing the outside linebacker position with his ability to rush the passer and drop into coverage. The success of the 3-4 defense in the 1980s prompted many teams to adopt or adapt the scheme, adding a new layer of complexity to defensive strategy.

The 1980s also saw a growing emphasis on **special teams** as a critical component of the game. Coaches began to recognize the impact that special teams could have on field position and momentum. This era saw the rise of specialized players, such as **kickoff and punt returners** who could change the course of a game with a single play. The importance of special teams was underscored by the success of players like **Billy "White Shoes" Johnson** and **Steve Tasker**, whose contributions in the return game and coverage units highlighted the strategic value of this often-overlooked aspect of football.

Offensively, the 1980s also witnessed the **evolution of the no-huddle offense**, which was used to great effect by the Cincinnati Bengals under head coach **Sam Wyche**. The no-huddle offense allowed teams to dictate the pace of the game, preventing defenses from making substitutions and forcing them to stay in basic formations. This strategy not only fatigued defenses but also created mismatches that offenses could exploit. The Bengals' success with the no-huddle offense, particularly in their run to Super Bowl XXIII, demonstrated its potential as a game-changing strategy.

Finally, the **advancement of defensive back play** in the 1980s also contributed to the strategic evolution of the game. As passing offenses became more sophisticated, defensive backs had to develop new techniques to keep up. The introduction of zone coverage schemes, such as the **Cover 2**, became more refined, allowing defenses to better defend against the deep pass while still providing strong support against the run. Players like **Ronnie Lott** of the San Francisco 49ers epitomized this evolution, combining physicality with exceptional coverage skills to become one of the most feared defenders of his era.

The strategic and schematic innovations of the 1980s were instrumental in shaping the modern NFL. Coaches and players alike pushed the boundaries of what was possible, leading to a more dynamic and complex game. These developments not only enhanced the competitive balance of the league but also made football more exciting and engaging for fans, setting the stage for the NFL's continued growth and popularity in the decades to come.

CHAPTER 10: THE 1990S - THE GLOBALIZATION OF THE NFL

Expansion Teams and Market Growth

The 1990s were a decade of significant expansion and market growth for the NFL, as the league sought to broaden its reach both domestically and internationally. This period was marked by the introduction of new teams, the relocation of existing franchises, and an ambitious push to make American football a global phenomenon.

One of the most notable aspects of the NFL's expansion during the 1990s was the addition of new teams. The league saw the debut of the **Carolina Panthers** and the **Jacksonville Jaguars** in 1995, marking the first time the NFL had added new franchises since 1976. The introduction of these teams was part of a broader strategy to tap into emerging markets in the southeastern United States, a region with a growing population and a strong interest in football. Both the Panthers and Jaguars quickly established themselves as competitive teams, reaching their respective conference championship games within their first few seasons. Their success on the field, coupled with strong fan support, demonstrated the viability of expanding the league into new markets.

In addition to the new franchises, the 1990s also saw significant relocations that reshaped the NFL's geographical landscape. The **Los Angeles Rams** moved to St. Louis in 1995, and the **Houston Oilers** relocated to Tennessee in 1997, eventually becoming the Tennessee Titans. These moves were driven by a combination of factors, including the pursuit of better stadium deals and the desire to tap into more lucrative markets. While controversial, these relocations were part of the NFL's broader strategy to maximize its market presence and ensure the financial stability of its franchises.

The 1990s were also marked by the NFL's efforts to expand its international footprint. The league launched the **NFL Europe** in 1991 (initially known as the World League of American Football), which served as both a developmental league for players and a platform to introduce American football to European audiences. Teams were based in cities like London, Barcelona, and Frankfurt, and the league enjoyed modest success in growing the sport's popularity overseas. Although NFL Europe was eventually discontinued in 2007, its existence in the 1990s was a key part of the NFL's strategy to globalize the game.

Domestically, the NFL continued to grow its market through increased television exposure and the development of new stadiums. The 1990s saw the construction of several state-of-the-art facilities, such as FedExField in Washington, D.C., and Raymond James Stadium in Tampa Bay, which helped enhance the fan experience and generate additional revenue streams. The league also benefited from lucrative television contracts, which ensured that NFL games reached a national audience and contributed to the league's continued financial success.

The expansion teams and market growth of the 1990s were crucial in shaping the modern NFL. By introducing new franchises, relocating teams to more promising markets, and expanding its global reach, the NFL laid the groundwork for its transformation into the dominant sports league it is today.

The Rise of the Dallas Cowboys Dynasty

The Dallas Cowboys of the 1990s emerged as one of the most dominant teams in NFL history, building a dynasty that captured three Super Bowl titles in four years. The foundation of this dynasty was laid in the late 1980s when **Jerry Jones** purchased the team and hired **Jimmy Johnson** as head coach. Together, they orchestrated one of the most impressive turnarounds in sports history, transforming the Cowboys from a struggling franchise into a powerhouse.

One of the keys to the Cowboys' success was their mastery of the NFL Draft. In 1989, the team made a bold move by trading away star running back **Herschel Walker** to the Minnesota Vikings in exchange for a bounty of draft picks. This trade, known as "The Great Train Robbery," provided the Cowboys with the assets needed to rebuild their roster. With these picks, the Cowboys selected future Hall of Famers like **Emmitt Smith**, **Troy Aikman**, and **Michael Irvin**, who would become the cornerstones of the team's success.

The Cowboys' offensive line, known as "The Great Wall of Dallas," was another critical component of their dominance. This unit, featuring Pro Bowlers like **Larry Allen** and **Nate Newton**, provided the protection and run-blocking that allowed Emmitt Smith to become the NFL's all-time leading rusher. Behind this line, Aikman's precision passing and Irvin's playmaking ability gave the Cowboys one of the most balanced and potent offenses in the league.

Defensively, the Cowboys were equally formidable. The unit, coordinated by **Dave Wannstedt** and later **Butch Davis**, was anchored by players like **Charles Haley**, **Darren Woodson**, and **Deion Sanders**. This defense was known for its physicality and ability to create turnovers, which often led to points for the offense.

The Cowboys' dominance was on full display in the early 1990s. They won Super Bowl XXVII in 1993 by defeating the Buffalo Bills 52-17, showcasing their explosive offense and opportunistic defense. They repeated as champions the following year in Super Bowl XXVIII, again defeating the Bills. After a brief setback in 1994, the Cowboys returned to the top in 1995, winning Super Bowl XXX against the Pittsburgh Steelers.

The success of the Dallas Cowboys in the 1990s was a result of shrewd management, excellent coaching, and the talent of their star players. This period cemented the Cowboys' legacy as "America's Team" and left an indelible mark on the NFL. Their dynasty set a standard for excellence that continues to influence the league today.

The Impact of Free Agency on the NFL

The introduction of free agency in the NFL in 1993 revolutionized the league, fundamentally altering the balance of power among teams and reshaping the way rosters were constructed. Before free agency, players had limited mobility, with teams holding almost total control over their contracts. The advent of free agency empowered players to negotiate with multiple teams once their contracts expired, leading to a more dynamic and competitive market for talent.

The origins of NFL free agency can be traced back to the landmark **Reggie White** case in 1992, when White, one of the league's premier defensive ends, became the first big-name player to test the new system. White's decision to sign with the Green Bay Packers was a game-changer, not just for the Packers, who gained a cornerstone player, but for the entire league. His move demonstrated the potential for free agency to help struggling teams quickly become contenders by acquiring top-tier talent.

Free agency introduced a new level of strategy into NFL team-building. Teams now had to balance their budgets carefully, deciding whether to invest in high-priced free agents or develop talent through the draft. The salary cap, which was also introduced in 1994, added another layer of complexity, forcing teams to make difficult decisions about which players to keep and which to let go. This dynamic created a more level playing field, as teams with smart management could quickly rebuild by making savvy free-agent signings.

One of the most significant impacts of free agency was the increased player movement across the league. Stars who had spent their entire careers with one team could now finish their careers elsewhere, often in pursuit of a championship. This movement not only changed the fortunes of teams but also altered fan loyalties, as players became less tied to a single franchise. The ability for players to choose their destinations also led to the formation of "super teams," where multiple stars would join forces to increase their chances of winning a Super Bowl.

Free agency also led to an increased emphasis on player performance and career longevity. Players were more motivated to perform at a high level throughout their contracts, knowing that their future earnings depended on their market value. This shift contributed to the overall improvement in the quality of play in the NFL, as the competition for contracts pushed players to maximize their potential.

Overall, the introduction of free agency in the 1990s had a profound impact on the NFL. It shifted the balance of power from teams to players, created a more competitive league, and changed the way teams approached roster construction. Free agency's influence on the NFL continues to be felt today, as it remains a key factor in shaping the league's competitive landscape.

International Games and NFL Europe

The 1990s marked a period of significant international expansion for the NFL, as the league sought to extend its reach beyond the United States and tap into new markets around the world. This effort was exemplified by the introduction of international games and the establishment of NFL Europe, both of which played crucial roles in the globalization of American football.

The NFL's first major step into the international arena came with the launch of the **American Bowl** series in 1986. These preseason games were held in cities around the world, including London, Tokyo, and Mexico City, and featured NFL teams playing in front of international audiences. The success of these games demonstrated the global appeal of American football and provided the NFL with valuable experience in organizing and promoting events outside the United States.

Building on the success of the American Bowl, the NFL established **NFL Europe** (originally called the World League of American Football) in 1991. NFL Europe served as both a developmental league for players and a platform for expanding the sport's popularity in Europe. Teams were based in cities like London, Frankfurt, and Barcelona, and the league operated as a spring counterpart to the NFL's fall season. NFL Europe provided a valuable opportunity for younger players to gain experience and for European fans to engage with the sport on a more consistent basis.

NFL Europe also introduced several innovations that were later adopted by the NFL, including the two-point conversion and the use of instant replay for officiating. These contributions, along with the league's role in developing talent, underscored its importance to the NFL's broader strategy of globalization.

Despite its contributions, NFL Europe faced several challenges, including financial losses and difficulty in sustaining fan interest over the long term. The league ultimately folded in 2007, but its legacy continued to influence the NFL's international strategy. The experiences gained from NFL Europe informed the

NFL's approach to international games, particularly the decision to schedule regular-season games abroad.

In 2007, the NFL began hosting regular-season games in London as part of the **International Series**, which proved to be highly successful. The games, held at Wembley Stadium and later at Tottenham Hotspur Stadium, consistently drew large crowds and showcased the NFL's commitment to growing its global footprint. The success of the London games led to the expansion of the International Series to other countries, including Mexico and Germany, further solidifying the NFL's presence on the world stage.

The NFL's international games and the establishment of NFL Europe were key milestones in the league's globalization efforts. While NFL Europe may no longer exist, its impact on the league's strategy and the growth of American football around the world is undeniable. Today, the NFL continues to build on these foundations, bringing the excitement of American football to fans across the globe.

The 1994 Salary Cap Introduction

The introduction of the salary cap in 1994 was a transformative moment in NFL history, fundamentally changing the way teams managed their rosters and finances. Before the salary cap, wealthier teams had a significant advantage, able to outspend smaller-market teams to acquire top talent. This imbalance threatened the competitive integrity of the league, as it created disparities that made it difficult for less affluent teams to compete.

The 1994 salary cap, set at $34.6 million per team, was designed to create a more level playing field. It forced teams to be more strategic in how they allocated their financial resources, balancing the need to pay star players while maintaining a competitive roster. The cap applied to all player salaries, bonuses, and incentives, ensuring that no team could monopolize talent simply by spending more money.

The introduction of the salary cap also made player contracts more complex. Teams had to consider not only the annual salary but also how signing bonuses and incentives would impact their cap space. This led to the rise of cap specialists within front offices, as teams needed experts to navigate the intricacies of the cap and maximize their roster's potential within financial constraints.

The salary cap has had a profound impact on the NFL, promoting parity and ensuring that every team has a fair chance to compete. It has made the league more competitive, as evidenced by the fact that since its introduction, multiple teams from both large and small markets have won Super Bowls. The salary cap remains a cornerstone of the NFL's financial structure, maintaining the competitive balance that has become a hallmark of the league.

The Introduction of Instant Replay

The introduction of instant replay in the NFL in 1986 marked a significant advancement in the officiating of the game, reflecting the league's commitment to accuracy and fairness. The initial version of instant replay was a limited system, designed to allow referees to review certain types of plays to ensure that crucial calls were made correctly. However, this early system was not without its challenges, including delays in the game and technical limitations that sometimes undermined its effectiveness.

Instant replay was initially met with mixed reactions from players, coaches, and fans. While many appreciated the added layer of accuracy it brought to officiating, others were frustrated by the interruptions it caused during games. The system was used intermittently and was even discontinued after the 1991 season due to these concerns. However, the demand for a more reliable system persisted, especially as the speed and complexity of the game increased.

In 1999, the NFL reintroduced instant replay with significant improvements. The new system allowed coaches to challenge two plays per game, with a third challenge awarded if the first two were successful. This version of instant replay was better integrated into the flow of the game, utilizing enhanced technology to provide clearer and faster reviews. The use of multiple camera angles and better communication between officials made the system more efficient and effective.

Since its reintroduction, instant replay has become an integral part of the NFL, helping to ensure that key plays are called correctly and reducing the impact of human error on the outcome of games. While it has evolved over the years, the core principle of instant replay—enhancing the fairness and integrity of the game—remains as vital as ever.

Strategic & Schematic Evolutions in the 1990s

The 1990s were a decade of significant strategic and schematic evolution in the NFL, as teams and coaches adapted to new rules, technologies, and player capabilities. These changes not only influenced the way the game was played but also laid the foundation for many of the strategies and systems still in use today.

One of the most notable strategic evolutions of the 1990s was the **increased emphasis on the passing game**. As the NFL continued to implement rules that favored offense—such as stricter enforcement of pass interference and holding penalties—teams began to focus more on aerial attacks. This shift was facilitated by the rise of quarterbacks like **Brett Favre**, **Steve Young**, and **Peyton Manning**, who excelled at reading defenses and delivering precise throws. Offensive coordinators developed more sophisticated passing schemes, incorporating complex route combinations and pre-snap motions to create mismatches and confuse defenses.

The 1990s also saw the **continued development of the West Coast Offense**, which had been popularized by Bill Walsh in the 1980s. This system, characterized by short, quick passes designed to control the clock and move the chains, became even more refined as coaches like **Mike Holmgren** and **Andy Reid** brought their own innovations to the scheme. The West Coast Offense's emphasis on timing, precision, and yards after catch (YAC) became a blueprint for many successful teams during the decade.

On the defensive side of the ball, the 1990s were marked by the **rise of the zone blitz**, a scheme that was particularly effective in countering the increasingly sophisticated passing offenses. The zone blitz, pioneered by coaches like **Dick LeBeau** of the Pittsburgh Steelers, combined elements of zone coverage with aggressive pass-rushing. By dropping defensive linemen into coverage while sending linebackers or defensive backs on blitzes, the zone blitz created confusion for opposing quarterbacks and allowed defenses to apply pressure without sacrificing coverage integrity. This innovation was a key factor in the success of defenses like the Steelers' "Blitzburgh" unit.

Another significant development in the 1990s was the **evolution of the running game**, particularly the use of the one-back, or single-back, formation. This formation, which often featured a lone running back without a fullback, allowed offenses to spread the field with additional wide receivers or tight ends, creating more space for the running back to operate. Running backs like **Barry Sanders** and **Emmitt Smith** thrived in these formations, using their vision and agility to exploit the gaps created by the spread-out defenses.

The 1990s also saw a growing emphasis on **special teams** as a strategic component of the game. Coaches began to recognize the importance of field position and the impact that kickoffs, punts, and returns could have on the outcome of games. This led to the rise of specialized players, such as return specialists and long snappers, whose roles were focused solely on executing in these critical areas.

Overall, the strategic and schematic evolutions of the 1990s were driven by a combination of rule changes, player talent, and coaching innovation. These developments not only made the game more exciting for fans but also increased the complexity and competitiveness of the NFL, setting the stage for the high-powered, fast-paced football that would define the league in the 21st century.

CHAPTER 11: THE 2000S - THE ERA OF PARITY

The Rise of the New England Patriots Dynasty

The rise of the New England Patriots as a dynasty in the 2000s is one of the most remarkable stories in NFL history. This era of dominance was characterized by strategic brilliance, a culture of discipline, and the extraordinary partnership between head coach **Bill Belichick** and quarterback **Tom Brady**.

The Patriots' ascent began in 2001, a year that started unremarkably but ended with the team's first Super Bowl victory. The season took a dramatic turn when starting quarterback **Drew Bledsoe** was injured early in the season, forcing the relatively unknown Tom Brady, a sixth-round draft pick in 2000, into the starting role. Under Belichick's guidance, Brady led the Patriots to an 11-5 record and an improbable playoff run. The Patriots capped the season with a stunning victory over the heavily favored St. Louis Rams in Super Bowl XXXVI, signaling the arrival of a new powerhouse in the NFL.

Belichick's defensive genius and Brady's poise under pressure became the hallmarks of the Patriots' success. The team's ability to adapt their game plan each week to exploit their opponents' weaknesses was a key factor in their dominance. Belichick's philosophy of placing team success over individual accolades fostered a culture of unselfishness and accountability, which became a cornerstone of the Patriots' dynasty.

The Patriots' success continued throughout the decade, with Super Bowl victories in 2003 and 2004. These back-to-back championships cemented their status as a dynasty and highlighted their consistency and resilience. In an era of free agency and salary caps, where maintaining long-term success was challenging, the Patriots defied the odds. They remained competitive year after year, with Brady emerging as one of the greatest quarterbacks of all time.

One of the most remarkable aspects of the Patriots' dynasty was their ability to thrive despite significant roster turnover. Belichick's talent for finding undervalued players and integrating them into his system was unmatched. Whether it was through the draft, trades, or free agency, the Patriots consistently brought in new talent that fit their team-first mentality.

The 2007 season was particularly notable, as the Patriots embarked on a historic undefeated regular season. Led by Brady's record-setting 50 touchdown passes, including 23 to newly acquired wide receiver **Randy Moss**, the Patriots dominated their opponents. However, their quest for perfection was halted by the New York Giants in Super Bowl XLII, one of the most shocking upsets in NFL history.

Despite the loss, the 2007 Patriots are still remembered as one of the greatest teams ever assembled.

The rise of the New England Patriots dynasty in the 2000s was a testament to the power of strategic innovation, leadership, and a relentless commitment to excellence. Belichick and Brady's partnership set the standard for success in the NFL, and their legacy continues to influence the game today. The Patriots' sustained dominance in an era of parity remains one of the most impressive achievements in the history of professional sports.

The Impact of Technology on the Game

The impact of technology on the NFL has been profound, transforming every aspect of the game, from how it is played and coached to how it is viewed by fans. In the 21st century, technology has become an integral part of the NFL, driving innovations that have enhanced both the on-field experience and the fan experience.

One of the most significant ways technology has influenced the game is through **video analysis**. Coaches and players now have access to advanced video tools that allow them to break down game footage in incredible detail. This has revolutionized game preparation, enabling teams to study opponents' tendencies, analyze individual player performances, and develop more sophisticated game plans. The use of tablets and other digital devices on the sidelines has also become commonplace, allowing players and coaches to review plays in real-time and make adjustments during the game.

The use of **instant replay** is another area where technology has transformed the game. While instant replay was first introduced in the 1980s, advancements in video technology have made it more accurate and reliable. High-definition cameras and sophisticated replay systems now allow officials to review plays from multiple angles, ensuring that crucial decisions are made with the highest degree of accuracy. The NFL has also introduced the SkyJudge system, where an official in the booth has access to replay technology and can assist with making or correcting calls on the field.

The Growth of Fantasy Football

The growth of fantasy football has been one of the most significant developments in the NFL's history, transforming how fans engage with the sport and contributing to the league's immense popularity. What began as a niche pastime in the 1960s has evolved into a multi-billion-dollar industry that attracts millions of players each year.

Fantasy football's origins can be traced back to 1962, when a group of sports enthusiasts in Oakland, California, created the first fantasy football league. The concept was simple: participants would draft real NFL players to form their own fantasy teams, earning points based on the players' performances in actual games. For many years, fantasy football remained a niche activity, enjoyed by a small but dedicated group of fans who manually tracked player statistics and calculated scores.

The advent of the internet in the 1990s revolutionized fantasy football, making it accessible to a much wider audience. Online platforms like Yahoo and ESPN began offering free fantasy football leagues, automating the scoring process and allowing participants to manage their teams with ease. This accessibility, combined with the explosion of NFL coverage on television and the internet, led to a rapid increase in the number of fantasy football players.

By the 2000s, fantasy football had become a cultural phenomenon. The NFL recognized its potential to engage fans and began to actively promote fantasy football through partnerships with media companies and the development of official fantasy football platforms. The league's investment paid off, as fantasy football helped to drive TV ratings, increase fan loyalty, and generate significant revenue through advertising and sponsorships.

Fantasy football's growth has also had a profound impact on how fans consume the NFL. Instead of focusing solely on their favorite teams, fantasy football players now have a vested interest in a wide range of games and players across the league. This has led to increased viewership of NFL games and more in-depth engagement with the sport. Fantasy football players often spend hours researching player stats, injury reports, and matchups, enhancing their understanding and appreciation of the game.

The rise of daily fantasy sports (DFS) in the 2010s further expanded the fantasy football landscape. Platforms like DraftKings and FanDuel introduced new ways to play, offering daily and weekly contests with cash prizes. DFS has attracted millions of players and has become a major component of the fantasy football industry.

The growth of fantasy football has had a lasting impact on the NFL, creating a more engaged and informed fan base. It has transformed the way fans interact with the sport, making every game, player, and statistic matter in a way that was unimaginable just a few decades ago. Fantasy football's popularity shows no signs of slowing down, continuing to be influential in the NFL's success.

The Changing Landscape of NFL Broadcasting

The landscape of NFL broadcasting has undergone significant changes in recent decades, driven by advances in technology and shifting viewer preferences. The 2000s saw the NFL embrace these changes, transforming how the game is delivered to fans and ensuring its continued dominance in the sports media landscape.

One of the most significant changes was the expansion of **television coverage**. The NFL began to offer more games in prime time, including the introduction of **Sunday Night Football** on NBC in 2006, which quickly became the most-watched television program in the United States. The league also extended its reach with the **NFL Network**, which began airing live games on Thursday nights, further increasing the availability of NFL content.

High-definition (HD) broadcasting also revolutionized the viewing experience, providing fans with clearer and more immersive coverage. The NFL was quick to adopt HD technology, enhancing the visual appeal of games and setting a new standard for sports broadcasting.

The growth of **digital and streaming platforms** in the 2000s added another layer to NFL broadcasting. The league partnered with companies like **DirecTV** for NFL Sunday Ticket, allowing fans to watch out-of-market games, and later embraced streaming services like **Amazon Prime Video** for Thursday Night Football. These innovations made it easier for fans to access games on multiple devices, catering to the growing demand for flexibility in how and where they watch football.

These changes in NFL broadcasting have not only expanded the league's audience but also set the stage for its continued evolution in the digital age.

Strategic & Schematic Evolutions in the 2000s

The 2000s were a decade of significant strategic and schematic evolution in the NFL, as teams adapted to new challenges and innovations in both offense and defense. The period was marked by a blend of traditional football concepts with modern strategies, leading to a more complex and dynamic game.

One of the most notable strategic developments of the 2000s was the **rise of the spread offense**. Originating from college football, the spread offense became increasingly popular in the NFL as teams sought to exploit mismatches in the passing game. The spread formation, often featuring four or five wide receivers and a single running back, stretched defenses horizontally, creating more space for quick, short passes. Quarterbacks like **Peyton Manning**, **Tom Brady**, and **Drew Brees** excelled in this system, using their quick decision-making and accuracy to pick apart defenses. The spread offense also incorporated elements of the West Coast Offense, emphasizing short, timing-based passes that allowed receivers to gain yards after the catch.

Another significant evolution was the **increased use of the shotgun formation**. While the shotgun had been around for decades, it became a staple in NFL offenses during the 2000s. The formation gave quarterbacks more time to read the defense and make decisions, which was particularly valuable in the era of fast, aggressive pass rushers. Teams like the New England Patriots and the Indianapolis Colts used the shotgun formation extensively, allowing their quarterbacks to orchestrate complex passing attacks with precision.

On the defensive side of the ball, the 2000s saw the **resurgence of the 3-4 defense**. This scheme, featuring three down linemen and four linebackers, provided greater flexibility in pass rushing and coverage. The 3-4 defense allowed teams to disguise their blitzes more effectively, creating confusion for opposing quarterbacks. The **Baltimore Ravens** and **Pittsburgh Steelers** were among the teams that mastered this defense, using it to dominate opponents with physical, opportunistic play.

The 2000s also witnessed the **rise of hybrid defenders**, players who could perform multiple roles on the field. These players, often a cross between a linebacker and a safety or a defensive end and a linebacker, allowed defenses to be more versatile and adaptive. **Troy Polamalu** of the Pittsburgh Steelers and **Brian Urlacher** of the Chicago Bears were prime examples of this trend, as their ability to cover, blitz, and support the run made them invaluable to their teams' defensive schemes.

The decade also saw an increased emphasis on **situational football**. Coaches like Bill Belichick of the New England Patriots became known for their ability to prepare their teams for specific game situations, such as two-minute drills, red zone efficiency, and third-down conversions. This focus on situational football allowed teams to maximize their chances of success in critical moments of the game.

Overall, the strategic and schematic evolutions of the 2000s were driven by a combination of offensive innovation, defensive adaptation, and a deeper understanding of situational play. These developments not only made the game more exciting and unpredictable but also set the stage for the continued evolution of football in the years to come.

CHAPTER 12: THE 2010S - SOCIAL ISSUES AND THE NFL

The NFL's Response to Concussions and CTE

The NFL's response to concussions and Chronic Traumatic Encephalopathy (CTE) became a central issue in the 2010s, as growing evidence linked the sport to long-term brain injuries. The league, under increasing scrutiny, had to address these concerns through a combination of policy changes, research initiatives, and public relations efforts.

The spotlight on concussions intensified after the publication of studies linking repeated head trauma in football to CTE, a degenerative brain disease. The research, notably by Dr. **Bennet Omalu**, highlighted the devastating effects of CTE on former NFL players, leading to symptoms like memory loss, depression, and cognitive decline. As public awareness grew, the NFL faced mounting pressure from players, families, and the media to take action.

In response, the NFL implemented several rule changes aimed at reducing the risk of head injuries. One of the most significant was the expansion of the **"defenseless player"** rule, which protected players from hits to the head and neck area, particularly during vulnerable moments like catching a pass. The league also introduced penalties for helmet-to-helmet contact, with the aim of discouraging dangerous tackling techniques.

Beyond rule changes, the NFL took steps to improve the management of concussions during games. The league mandated the presence of independent neurological consultants on the sidelines to evaluate players suspected of having a concussion. These consultants had the authority to remove players from the game, ensuring that medical decisions were made with player safety as the priority. The NFL also introduced the **concussion protocol**, a standardized process that players had to go through before being allowed to return to play, involving multiple stages of evaluation and rest.

The NFL's commitment to addressing concussions extended to research. In 2016, the league pledged $100 million to fund independent research into head injuries and to develop better protective equipment. This initiative included partnerships with institutions like **Boston University's CTE Center**, which conducted in-depth studies on the brains of deceased players. The findings from these studies were crucial in advancing the understanding of CTE and its connection to football.

However, the NFL's response was not without criticism. Many argued that the league had been slow to acknowledge the severity of the issue and that the measures taken were insufficient to protect players. The 2013 settlement of a lawsuit filed by former players, who claimed the NFL had concealed the dangers of concussions, highlighted the deep mistrust between the league and its players. Although the settlement provided compensation for affected players, it also underscored the ongoing tensions surrounding the issue.

The NFL's response to concussions and CTE in the 2010s was a complex mix of proactive measures and reactive strategies. While the league made significant strides in addressing the problem, the long-term impact of these efforts remains a subject of intense debate. The issue of player safety continues to evolve, reflecting the ongoing challenge of balancing the sport's inherent risks with the well-being of its athletes.

The Rise of Player Activism

The 2010s witnessed a significant rise in player activism in the NFL, as athletes increasingly used their platform to address social and political issues. This movement was most prominently symbolized by **Colin Kaepernick**, the San Francisco 49ers quarterback who, in 2016, began kneeling during the national anthem to protest police brutality and racial inequality. Kaepernick's protest sparked a national conversation, with many players across the league joining him in various forms of protest, such as raising fists or locking arms.

Kaepernick's actions, while polarizing, highlighted the growing willingness of NFL players to speak out on issues beyond the football field. The support from players, both current and retired, underscored a shift in the culture of professional sports, where athletes were no longer content to remain silent on social justice matters. This period also saw players organizing community outreach programs, participating in voter registration drives, and engaging in discussions about criminal justice reform.

The NFL's response to player activism evolved over time. Initially, the league faced criticism for its handling of the protests, particularly as Kaepernick found himself without a team after the 2016 season. However, as the decade progressed, the NFL began to support players' efforts more openly, launching initiatives like the **Inspire Change** program, which aimed to address social justice issues and support community programs.

The rise of player activism in the 2010s marked a new era in the NFL, where athletes asserted their influence beyond the gridiron, advocating for change and using their voices to address pressing societal issues.

The Expansion of the Regular Season

The expansion of the NFL regular season from 16 to 17 games in 2021 was a significant development in the league's history, marking the first major change to the season structure since 1978. This move, part of the new collective bargaining agreement (CBA) between the NFL and the NFL Players Association (NFLPA), reflected the league's ongoing efforts to grow its brand and increase revenue, while also addressing the demands of a modern, global fanbase.

The decision to expand the regular season was driven largely by financial considerations. Adding an extra game to the schedule provided the NFL with additional opportunities for revenue generation through ticket sales, broadcasting rights, and advertising. The 17th game also allowed the league to schedule more international games, supporting its strategy of expanding the NFL's global footprint.

However, the expansion was not without controversy. Players and critics raised concerns about the potential impact on player health and safety. An additional game in an already grueling season increased the risk of injuries and extended the physical toll on players. To mitigate these concerns, the NFL reduced the preseason from four games to three, allowing players more time to recover and prepare for the regular season.

Despite the challenges, the expansion of the regular season was seen as a natural evolution of the NFL, aligning with the league's goals of growth and global reach. The additional game has created new dynamics in playoff races and historical records, adding another layer of intrigue to the NFL's ever-competitive landscape. As the league continues to evolve, the 17-game season is likely to remain a key component of its strategy moving forward.

Strategic & Schematic Evolutions in the 2010s

The 2010s were a decade of significant strategic and schematic evolution in the NFL, as the game continued to evolve in response to changing rules, player abilities, and coaching philosophies. This period saw the refinement of offensive and defensive strategies that reshaped how teams approached the game, leading to an era defined by innovation and adaptation.

One of the most prominent developments in the 2010s was the **proliferation of the spread offense**. Building on concepts from college football, the spread offense became a staple in the NFL, with teams like the Kansas City Chiefs and the Philadelphia Eagles utilizing formations that spread the defense horizontally across the field. This approach created more space for quick, short passes, allowing quarterbacks to exploit mismatches and put pressure on defenses. The rise of mobile quarterbacks, such as **Russell Wilson** and **Lamar Jackson**, further enhanced the effectiveness of the spread offense, as their ability to run and pass with equal proficiency forced defenses to account for multiple threats.

The decade also saw the **increased use of run-pass option (RPO) plays**, which blurred the traditional lines between running and passing plays. RPOs gave quarterbacks the flexibility to make decisions after the snap, based on the defense's reaction. This innovation, popularized by teams like the Philadelphia Eagles during their Super Bowl LII run, added a layer of unpredictability to offenses and made defending the run and pass simultaneously more challenging for defenses.

On the defensive side, the 2010s were marked by the rise of **hybrid defenses** and versatile players who could fill multiple roles. Defenses increasingly relied on players who could both cover and rush the passer, such as **Von Miller** and **Khalil Mack**. These hybrid defenders allowed defensive coordinators to disguise their schemes and create confusion for opposing quarterbacks. The Seattle Seahawks' **"Legion of Boom"** defense, coordinated by **Dan Quinn**, exemplified this trend, with a secondary that combined physicality with the ability to cover large areas of the field.

The **shift towards smaller, faster linebackers** also defined the 2010s, as defenses adapted to the increasingly pass-heavy nature of the NFL. Traditional, bulky linebackers were gradually replaced by more agile players who could cover tight ends and running backs in space. This evolution was necessary to keep up with offenses that relied on quick passes and spread formations. Teams like the Los Angeles Rams and the New England Patriots were at the forefront of this shift, utilizing speed and versatility in their linebacker corps to counter modern offenses.

Another significant development in the 2010s was the emphasis on **situational football** and analytics. Coaches like **Bill Belichick** and **Sean McVay** became known for their meticulous preparation and use of data to inform in-game decisions. The use of analytics to guide fourth-down decisions, play-calling tendencies, and clock management became increasingly prevalent, leading to more calculated and efficient game plans.

The 2010s also saw a growing reliance on **pre-snap motion and shifts**, which allowed offenses to gain insights into defensive coverages and create favorable matchups. This tactic, used effectively by teams like the San Francisco 49ers under **Kyle Shanahan**, kept defenses off balance and opened up opportunities for big plays.

The strategic and schematic evolutions of the 2010s were driven by a combination of innovation, adaptation, and the relentless pursuit of competitive advantage. These changes not only made the game more exciting for fans but also pushed the boundaries of what was possible on the football field, setting the stage for continued evolution in the 2020s and beyond.

CHAPTER 13: THE MODERN NFL (2020-PRESENT)

The Impact of the COVID-19 Pandemic

The COVID-19 pandemic had a profound impact on the NFL, forcing the league to navigate unprecedented challenges during the 2020 season. The pandemic tested the NFL's resilience, adaptability, and commitment to player and fan safety, ultimately reshaping how the league operates.

As the virus spread globally, the NFL faced the daunting task of conducting a full season amid a public health crisis. The league responded by implementing strict health and safety protocols. Daily testing for players, coaches, and staff became mandatory, and teams were required to follow rigorous guidelines to minimize the risk of infection. The NFL also developed a contact tracing system to quickly identify and isolate individuals who had been exposed to the virus.

One of the most visible changes was the absence of fans in the stands. Many teams played their home games in empty or sparsely populated stadiums, dramatically altering the atmosphere of NFL games. The usual roar of the crowd was replaced by artificial crowd noise, and teams had to adjust to playing in an environment devoid of the energy that typically comes from a full stadium. This shift affected home-field advantage, as the lack of crowd noise made communication easier for visiting teams.

The pandemic also forced the NFL to be flexible with its schedule. Several games were postponed or rescheduled due to outbreaks within teams, leading to a chaotic season where teams had to prepare for opponents on short notice. The league's ability to adapt its schedule, including playing games on nearly every day of the week, was crucial in completing the season without canceling any games.

Financially, the pandemic dealt a significant blow to the NFL. The loss of ticket revenue, coupled with reduced concessions and merchandise sales, impacted the league's overall earnings. To mitigate the financial strain, the NFL and the NFL Players Association (NFLPA) agreed to spread out the economic impact over several years, adjusting the salary cap to account for the reduced revenue.

Despite these challenges, the NFL successfully completed the 2020 season, culminating in Super Bowl LV. The game, played in front of a limited crowd in Tampa, Florida, was a testament to the league's ability to adapt in the face of adversity. The pandemic also accelerated the NFL's adoption of technology, with virtual meetings, remote scouting, and digital fan engagement becoming more commonplace.

The impact of the COVID-19 pandemic on the NFL was profound, forcing the league to rethink its operations and make significant adjustments. The 2020 season will be remembered not only for its on-field performances but also for the resilience and adaptability shown by the league in navigating one of the most challenging periods in its history.

The NFL's Embrace of Technology and Data Analytics

The NFL's embrace of technology and data analytics has revolutionized how teams prepare for games, manage players, and strategize on the field. Over the past decade, the integration of advanced technologies has become essential to the league's operations, enhancing both performance and fan engagement.

One of the most significant developments in this area has been the use of **Next Gen Stats**, a system that uses RFID chips embedded in players' uniforms and the football itself to track movement in real time. This technology provides teams with detailed data on player speed, acceleration, distance covered, and positioning. Coaches and analysts use this information to make more informed decisions, from play-calling to player conditioning. It also allows teams to identify tendencies and optimize game strategies based on concrete, real-time data.

Data analytics has also transformed player evaluation and recruitment. Teams now rely on sophisticated algorithms to assess player performance and potential, going beyond traditional statistics. These tools analyze vast amounts of data to identify undervalued players, predict injury risks, and tailor training programs to individual needs. This analytical approach has led to smarter drafting and more efficient roster management, giving teams a competitive edge.

On the fan engagement front, the NFL has integrated technology to enhance the viewing experience. Augmented reality (AR), virtual reality (VR), and advanced graphics are now commonplace in broadcasts, providing fans with deeper insights into the game. Additionally, fantasy football platforms and betting apps leverage real-time data, keeping fans engaged and connected to the action.

The NFL's commitment to technology and data analytics has not only improved on-field performance but also deepened fan engagement, making the game more dynamic and accessible than ever before.

Ongoing Rule Changes and Safety Measures

The NFL has continually evolved its rules and safety measures to address the changing nature of the game and ensure player safety. In recent years, the league has implemented several key rule changes aimed at reducing injuries, particularly those related to head trauma, while maintaining the sport's competitive integrity.

One of the most significant ongoing changes has been the expansion of the **targeting rule**. The NFL has made it a priority to protect players from head injuries by penalizing hits that involve helmet-to-helmet contact or hits to the head and neck area of a defenseless player. This rule is strictly enforced, with players facing fines, suspensions, and even ejections for violations. The league's focus on reducing concussions has also led to improvements in helmet technology and stricter protocols for managing concussed players.

The NFL has also adjusted rules related to **kickoffs and punts**, two of the most dangerous plays in football. To reduce the high-speed collisions that often occur during these plays, the league moved the kickoff line and restricted the running start of coverage teams. These changes have led to more touchbacks and fewer returns, which in turn has decreased the number of injuries on special teams.

In addition to player safety, the NFL has introduced rule changes to maintain the pace and excitement of the game. The adoption of the **overtime rules**, which guarantee each team at least one possession in playoff games, reflects the league's commitment to fairness and competitive balance.

The NFL's ongoing rule changes and safety measures demonstrate the league's proactive approach to protecting its players while ensuring that the game remains engaging and competitive. As the sport continues to evolve, the NFL's focus on safety and fairness will likely drive further innovations in its rules and regulations.

The Global Expansion Strategy

The NFL's global expansion strategy is a key component of its long-term vision to grow the sport's popularity beyond the United States. Recognizing the potential of untapped markets, the league has implemented a multi-faceted approach that includes international games, grassroots initiatives, and strategic partnerships to bring American football to a global audience.

One of the cornerstones of the NFL's global strategy is the **International Series**, which began in 2007 with regular-season games held in London. These games, played at iconic venues like Wembley Stadium and Tottenham Hotspur Stadium, have been hugely successful, consistently drawing large crowds and generating significant media attention. The success of the London games led the NFL to expand the series to other locations, including Mexico City and, more recently, Germany. These international games serve as both a showcase for the sport and a way to build a fan base in key global markets.

In addition to the International Series, the NFL has invested in **grassroots programs** to cultivate a love for the game among young athletes in other countries. The league has launched initiatives like NFL Flag Football and the NFL Academy in the UK, which aim to introduce American football to a younger audience and develop local talent. These programs are designed to build a foundation for the sport at the grassroots level, with the hope that increased participation will lead to greater interest and viewership over time.

The NFL has also focused on **strategic partnerships** to expand its global reach. Collaborations with broadcasters, streaming platforms, and digital media companies have allowed the NFL to deliver its content to a global audience more effectively. The league's partnership with Sky Sports in the UK, for example, has made NFL games more accessible to British fans, while deals with streaming services like DAZN have expanded the league's presence in markets like Canada, Germany, and Japan. These partnerships are crucial for the NFL's strategy to reach new fans and grow its brand internationally.

Moreover, the NFL has recognized the importance of tailoring its product to fit local markets. This has included the introduction of localized content, such as NFL broadcasts in multiple languages and the development of region-specific digital content. The league has also explored the idea of establishing a permanent franchise in London, which would mark a significant step in its global expansion efforts. While this remains a complex and ambitious goal, the consistent success of the International Series suggests that such an endeavor could be viable in the future.

The NFL's global expansion strategy also includes leveraging its most marketable assets: the players. The league has encouraged international players to join the NFL through programs like the **International Player Pathway Program**, which provides opportunities for athletes from outside the U.S. to train and compete in the NFL. Players like **Efe Obada** and **Jakob Johnson**, who came through this program, have become ambassadors for the sport in their home countries, helping to raise the NFL's profile globally.

The Future of the NFL

The future of the NFL is poised to be shaped by a combination of technological innovation, global expansion, and evolving player safety measures. As the league continues to grow, its ability to adapt to changing times will be key to maintaining its position as the premier professional sports league in the world.

Technology will play a central role in the NFL's future. The integration of artificial intelligence (AI) and machine learning could revolutionize game analysis, player training, and injury prevention. Wearable technology will likely become more advanced, providing real-time data that can enhance player performance and health management. Virtual and augmented reality could also transform the fan experience, offering immersive ways to engage with games, whether in stadiums or from home.

Global expansion remains a top priority for the NFL. The success of international games in London, Mexico City, and Germany has demonstrated the sport's growing global appeal. The league is likely to continue exploring new markets, with potential for establishing permanent franchises outside the United States. This expansion will be supported by increased digital content tailored to international audiences, making the NFL more accessible to fans worldwide.

Player safety will continue to be a major focus, as the NFL seeks to address concerns about concussions and other injuries. Ongoing research into helmet technology, as well as rule changes designed to protect players, will be crucial in ensuring the game's sustainability. The league's efforts to reduce injury risks will also extend to youth and amateur football, promoting safer play from the grassroots level.

As the NFL looks to the future, its ability to innovate, expand globally, and prioritize player safety will be critical to its continued success and relevance in an ever-changing sports landscape.

Strategic & Schematic Evolutions in the 2020s

The 2020s have ushered in a new era of strategic and schematic evolution in the NFL, driven by advancements in technology, rule changes, and the continued development of player skills. As offenses become more dynamic and defenses more adaptable, the game continues to evolve in ways that challenge traditional football norms.

One of the most notable developments in the 2020s is the **further integration of analytics into game strategy**. Teams increasingly rely on data-driven insights to inform decisions on play-calling, fourth-down attempts, and player usage. This analytical approach has led to more aggressive strategies, such as going for it on fourth down in situations that would have traditionally called for a punt or field goal attempt. Coaches like **Brandon Staley** of the Los Angeles Chargers and **Kevin Stefanski** of the Cleveland Browns have embraced this data-driven mindset, pushing the boundaries of conventional football wisdom.

Offensively, the **evolution of the passing game** has continued to dominate the strategic landscape. The 2020s have seen an even greater emphasis on **quick-release passing** and **pre-snap motion**, designed to create mismatches and exploit defensive tendencies. Quarterbacks are expected to process information rapidly and deliver the ball with precision, often targeting multiple receivers in quick succession.

This approach has been epitomized by quarterbacks like **Patrick Mahomes** and **Josh Allen**, whose ability to make plays both in and out of the pocket has redefined what is possible at the position. The talent level at the quarterback position has grown significantly.

The rise of **positionless football** has also been a significant trend. Offensive coordinators are increasingly using versatile players who can line up in multiple positions, creating confusion for defenses. Players like **Deebo Samuel** of the San Francisco 49ers, who can function as both a wide receiver and a running back, embody this trend. This flexibility allows offenses to disguise their intentions and keep defenses guessing, leading to more creative and unpredictable play-calling.

Defensively, the 2020s have seen the **continued development of hybrid defenses** that blend elements of traditional schemes with modern innovations. Teams are increasingly using defensive backs who can play both cornerback and safety, as well as linebackers who can rush the passer, cover receivers, and stop the run. The use of **disguised coverages** and **post-snap rotations** has become more prevalent, with defenses attempting to confuse quarterbacks by showing one look before the snap and shifting into another after the play begins. This has made it more difficult for even the most experienced quarterbacks to anticipate and exploit defensive weaknesses.

The importance of **defensive speed** has also been magnified in the 2020s. As offenses continue to prioritize speed and agility, defenses have had to respond by fielding faster, more athletic players who can cover large areas of the field and make plays in space. This shift has led to a reduction in the size of traditional linebackers and an increase in the use of faster, more versatile defenders who can keep up with the pace of modern offenses.

Another key evolution in the 2020s has been the **increased use of sub-packages** on defense. Rather than sticking with a base defense, teams now frequently rotate in specialized personnel based on down and distance, creating tailored responses to specific offensive formations and play calls. This strategic flexibility allows defenses to better match up against the increasingly complex offensive schemes they face.

Overall, the strategic and schematic evolutions of the 2020s reflect a game that is more fluid, dynamic, and data-driven than ever before.

CHAPTER 14: THE NFL'S CULTURAL INFLUENCE

The NFL's Role in American Pop Culture

The NFL's role in American pop culture is profound, deeply woven into the fabric of the nation's identity. The league has transcended sports to become a significant cultural force, influencing everything from fashion and music to television and politics.

One of the most visible aspects of the NFL's cultural influence is the **Super Bowl**, an event that has become much more than a football game. It's a national spectacle that captures the attention of millions, including those who don't typically follow sports. The Super Bowl halftime show, featuring performances by the world's biggest musical acts, is a prime example of how the NFL intersects with the entertainment industry. These performances, watched by millions worldwide, often set trends in music and fashion, reflecting and shaping contemporary culture.

NFL players themselves have become cultural icons, influencing public discourse and popular trends. Figures like **Tom Brady**, **Odell Beckham Jr.**, and **Patrick Mahomes** have not only excelled on the field but have also become influential off it. Their endorsement deals, social media presence, and participation in mainstream media have made them household names, with their actions and opinions resonating far beyond the football field.

The NFL's impact extends into **fashion and merchandise** as well. The popularity of team jerseys, hats, and other gear has made NFL merchandise a staple in American wardrobes. The league's ability to market its brands has turned team logos and colors into symbols of identity and community, worn proudly by fans across the country.

Television has was key in embedding the NFL in American culture. NFL games are consistently among the highest-rated programs on TV, and the league has mastered the art of broadcasting, turning games into must-watch events. The proliferation of NFL-themed content, from documentaries to reality shows, has further solidified its presence in the media landscape. Shows like "Hard Knocks" give fans a behind-the-scenes look at teams, deepening their connection to the sport.

Moreover, the NFL's influence can be seen in **language and everyday conversation**. Terms like "Hail Mary," "Monday Morning Quarterback," and "blitz" have entered the American lexicon, used in contexts far removed from football. This linguistic influence underscores how deeply the NFL is ingrained in the national consciousness.

The league has also played a significant role in **social and political movements**. NFL players have used their platforms to advocate for change, from the civil rights movements of the past to more recent protests against racial injustice. These actions have sparked national conversations and highlighted the NFL's position as a powerful cultural institution that can influence public opinion.

The Influence of NFL Films and Media

NFL Films has played a pivotal role in shaping how football is viewed, understood, and celebrated in American culture. Since its founding in 1962 by **Ed Sabol** and his son **Steve Sabol**, NFL Films has transformed the way the sport is documented, turning football games into cinematic experiences that capture the drama, emotion, and artistry of the game.

The hallmark of NFL Films is its distinctive style. Through the use of slow-motion replays, dramatic music, and poetic narration, NFL Films has elevated football from a mere sport to a form of storytelling. This approach has given fans a deeper appreciation for the game, highlighting the athleticism and strategy involved in each play. The narration, often delivered by the iconic voice of **John Facenda**, known as the "Voice of God," adds a gravitas that makes each moment feel epic, regardless of the game's stakes.

NFL Films has also been instrumental in building the mythology around the NFL's greatest players and moments. By focusing on the human side of the sport, NFL Films has created enduring images of legends like **Vince Lombardi**, **Joe Namath**, and **Walter Payton**. These films have not only preserved the history of the game but have also contributed to the larger-than-life personas of its stars.

Moreover, NFL Films has influenced the broader sports media landscape. Its techniques have been emulated by other sports leagues and broadcasters, setting a standard for how sports are visually presented. The ability of NFL Films to evoke emotion and tell compelling stories has made it a cornerstone of the NFL's brand, helping to deepen fans' connection to the sport.

In addition to its influence on visual storytelling, NFL Films has contributed significantly to the NFL's marketing efforts. The company's documentaries, highlight reels, and weekly programs like "NFL Films Presents" and "Inside the NFL" have been essential in promoting the league, both in the United States and internationally. By showcasing the drama and excitement of football, NFL Films has played a key role in expanding the NFL's fan base and maintaining its status as the most popular sport in America.

Football as a Thanksgiving Tradition

Football and Thanksgiving have become inseparable in American culture, with the tradition of NFL games on Thanksgiving Day dating back to the early days of the league. This annual event has turned Thanksgiving into more than just a holiday for gathering and feasting; it has become a day when families and friends unite around the television to watch football, making it a central part of the celebration.

The tradition began in 1934 when the **Detroit Lions** hosted the **Chicago Bears** in the first NFL game played on Thanksgiving. The game was the brainchild of Lions' owner **G.A. Richards**, who wanted to boost attendance for his team. The idea proved successful, drawing a large crowd and generating significant national attention. Since then, the Lions have played on Thanksgiving every year, becoming a fixture of the holiday.

In 1966, the **Dallas Cowboys** joined the tradition, hosting their first Thanksgiving game. The Cowboys, known as "America's Team," quickly turned their Thanksgiving Day games into a major spectacle, drawing huge television audiences and further embedding football into the fabric of the holiday. The Cowboys' participation cemented the connection between Thanksgiving and football, with millions of Americans tuning in each year to watch the games.

In recent years, the NFL has added a third Thanksgiving game, played in prime time, allowing fans to enjoy football from midday through the evening. These games have become an integral part of the Thanksgiving experience, offering a mix of tradition and excitement that complements the holiday's spirit of togetherness.

Football on Thanksgiving has become more than just a sports event, but a cultural ritual that brings people together. Whether fans are rooting for their favorite team or simply enjoying the competition, the games provide a shared experience that adds to the warmth and camaraderie of the holiday. The NFL's Thanksgiving games are a reminder of how deeply football is woven into the traditions of American life, making it a day of celebration both on and off the field.

The Super Bowl Halftime Show and Advertisements

The Super Bowl halftime show and its advertisements have evolved into cultural phenomena that extend far beyond the game itself. While the Super Bowl has long been the pinnacle of American football, the halftime show and commercials have become central to its allure, drawing in viewers who might not even be football fans.

The halftime show, initially a modest affair featuring marching bands, has transformed into a spectacular showcase of the world's top musical talents. This shift began in earnest in the early 1990s when the NFL decided to make the halftime show a centerpiece of the Super Bowl experience. The turning point came with **Michael Jackson's** performance in 1993, which set the standard for the extravagant, high-energy shows that now define the event. Today, the halftime show is a must-watch, featuring elaborate stage productions, surprise guest appearances, and memorable performances from artists like **Beyoncé**, **Prince**, and **Lady Gaga**. The show's influence extends beyond the live audience, often setting trends in music, fashion, and entertainment.

Equally significant are the advertisements aired during the Super Bowl, which have become as much a part of the event as the game itself. Companies pay millions of dollars for a 30-second spot, knowing that the Super Bowl offers them an unparalleled opportunity to reach a massive and engaged audience. These commercials are often highly anticipated, with brands going all out to create ads that are funny, emotional, or innovative. Some Super Bowl ads have become iconic, remembered and discussed long after the game ends. The buzz around these commercials often starts weeks before the Super Bowl, with teasers and social media campaigns adding to the excitement.

The importance of the Super Bowl halftime show and advertisements highlights how the event transcends sports, becoming a major cultural event that captures the attention of the entire country. For many, the halftime show and commercials are as eagerly anticipated as the game itself, reflecting the Super Bowl's unique place in American culture.

The NFL's Impact on Youth and College Football

The NFL's influence extends deeply into youth and college football, shaping how the game is played and perceived at all levels. The league's impact is seen in the widespread popularity of football among young athletes, the development of talent pipelines, and the implementation of safety standards that are changing the sport from the ground up.

Youth football programs across the United States serve as the entry point for many young athletes who aspire to play in the NFL. The popularity of the NFL fuels interest in the sport, encouraging kids to join teams and develop their skills at an early age. Programs like **Pop Warner** and **USA Football's Heads Up Football** initiative provide structured environments where young players can learn the fundamentals of the game while also emphasizing safety and sportsmanship. The NFL's promotion of these programs has been crucial in maintaining football's status as America's most popular sport.

In college football, the NFL's influence is perhaps most evident in the development of players. College football serves as a critical training ground for future NFL stars, with many universities investing heavily in their football programs. The NFL's annual draft, which selects the top college players, is a major event that highlights the close relationship between the college and professional levels. College coaches often model their programs after NFL teams, incorporating professional-level strategies, training regimens, and playbooks to prepare their athletes for the next step in their careers.

The NFL has also driven significant changes in how football is coached and played at the youth and college levels, particularly concerning safety. As concerns about concussions and injuries have grown, the NFL has promoted safer tackling techniques and equipment improvements, influencing how the game is taught to young players. These changes are designed to protect players' health and ensure that the sport remains viable and safe for future generations.

The NFL's impact on youth and college football is profound, as it not only fosters the next generation of talent but also shapes the very structure of the sport. The league's influence ensures that football remains a key part of American life, from the local youth leagues to the grand stage of the NFL.

CHAPTER 15: THE ECONOMICS OF THE NFL

The Business of NFL Broadcasting Rights

The business of NFL broadcasting rights is a cornerstone of the league's financial success, driving billions of dollars in revenue and having an important role in the league's growth. The NFL's ability to command top dollar for its television rights has not only made it the richest sports league in the world but also ensured its games are a fixture in American culture.

The foundation of the NFL's broadcasting success was laid in the 1960s, when Commissioner **Pete Rozelle** recognized the potential of television to grow the sport. Rozelle's vision led to the landmark 1961 Sports Broadcasting Act, which allowed the NFL to negotiate television rights as a single entity. This was a game-changer. Instead of individual teams negotiating their own deals, the league could leverage its collective power to secure national contracts, ensuring all teams benefited equally from television revenue.

The NFL's first major television deal came in 1962 when CBS agreed to pay $4.65 million annually for the rights to broadcast NFL games. This was just the beginning. Over the decades, the value of NFL broadcasting rights skyrocketed, reflecting the league's growing popularity. By the 1990s, the NFL was signing multi-billion dollar contracts with networks like CBS, NBC, Fox, and ESPN, each vying for a piece of the NFL's massive audience.

Today, the NFL's broadcasting rights are among the most lucrative in sports. In 2021, the NFL signed a 10-year, $113 billion deal with its broadcast partners, including CBS, NBC, Fox, ESPN, and Amazon. This deal, the largest in sports history, guarantees the NFL a staggering $10 billion per year, underscoring the league's unrivaled power in the television landscape.

What makes these deals so valuable is the NFL's consistent ability to deliver large, live audiences. In an era where streaming and on-demand viewing have fragmented television audiences, live sports—especially NFL games—remain a rare commodity that attracts millions of viewers in real-time. Advertisers are willing to pay a premium to reach these viewers, and networks are eager to capitalize on this demand.

The NFL has also been at the forefront of embracing new technologies and platforms. The inclusion of Amazon in the latest broadcast deal highlights the league's recognition of the shifting media landscape. Streaming services represent a growing share of how audiences consume content, and the NFL's willingness to partner with digital platforms ensures that it remains accessible to younger, tech-savvy viewers.

Beyond television, the revenue generated from broadcasting rights fuels the entire NFL ecosystem. The income supports player salaries, funds stadium improvements, and allows for the expansion of league initiatives. It also contributes to the revenue-sharing model that helps maintain competitive balance among teams.

The business of NFL broadcasting rights is a masterclass in how to maximize the value of a sports product. The league's strategic negotiation of these deals has ensured its financial dominance, while also reinforcing football's place at the heart of American entertainment. As the media landscape continues to evolve, the NFL's approach to broadcasting rights will likely remain a critical factor in its sustained success.

The NFL's Revenue Sharing Model

The NFL's revenue-sharing model is a cornerstone of the league's financial structure, designed to promote competitive balance and ensure the long-term viability of all 32 teams, regardless of market size. This system allows the NFL to distribute its vast earnings in a way that keeps the playing field level and the league strong.

At the heart of the revenue-sharing model is the collective bargaining of **television broadcasting rights**. The NFL negotiates national TV deals as a single entity, rather than allowing individual teams to strike their own deals. The revenue from these multi-billion-dollar contracts is then divided equally among all teams. This means that even teams in smaller markets, like Green Bay or Buffalo, receive the same share of TV revenue as teams in large markets like New York or Los Angeles. This equal distribution is crucial for maintaining competitive balance, as it prevents wealthier teams from outspending their rivals on player salaries and other expenses.

In addition to broadcasting rights, the NFL also shares revenue from national sponsorships, licensing deals, and merchandise sales. For example, the league's agreement with companies like Nike and Pepsi generates significant income, which is pooled and distributed equally among the teams. This approach ensures that all teams benefit from the league's commercial success, regardless of their individual performance or market size.

However, not all revenue in the NFL is shared equally. Teams retain the majority of their local revenue, including ticket sales, concessions, and local sponsorships. This allows teams to benefit from strong local support and incentivizes them to invest in their fan experience and stadium facilities. Despite this, the shared national revenue is substantial enough to support smaller-market teams and keep the league competitive.

The revenue-sharing model has been pivotal in the NFL's growth into the most financially successful sports league in the world. It has helped prevent the large disparities in wealth that have plagued other leagues and has ensured that every team has the financial resources to compete effectively. This system not only underpins the league's stability but also contributes to its broad appeal, as fans know that their team, no matter how small the market, has a fair chance of success.

The Economic Impact of Hosting an NFL Team

Hosting an NFL team can have a significant economic impact on a city, influencing everything from local business revenue to infrastructure development. While the benefits can be substantial, the true economic impact is often a subject of debate, as the costs and rewards can vary widely depending on the circumstances.

One of the most immediate benefits of hosting an NFL team is the **boost to local businesses**. On game days, stadiums attract tens of thousands of fans, many of whom spend money on parking, dining, and shopping. This influx of visitors provides a steady stream of revenue for local businesses, particularly those located near the stadium. Bars, restaurants, and hotels often see a significant increase in business during the NFL season, especially in cities with passionate fan bases.

Another major economic benefit comes from **job creation**. The presence of an NFL team supports a wide range of jobs, from stadium staff and security to hospitality workers and local vendors. Additionally, the construction or renovation of a stadium can create thousands of jobs, both temporary and permanent, contributing to the local economy. The ongoing operation of the stadium and the team also requires a large workforce, providing employment opportunities in various sectors.

However, the economic impact of hosting an NFL team is not without its challenges. The cost of building and maintaining a modern NFL stadium can be enormous, often requiring significant public funding. Cities frequently subsidize stadium construction through tax increases or public bonds, leading to debates over whether the long-term economic benefits justify the upfront costs. Critics argue that the promised economic boosts are often overstated, and that public money could be better spent on other infrastructure or community projects.

Despite these concerns, many cities view hosting an NFL team as a matter of prestige and community pride, beyond just the financial returns. The presence of a team can enhance a city's national profile, attract tourists, and serve as a focal point for civic identity. The potential for hosting major events like the Super Bowl also adds to the appeal, as these events bring significant economic activity and media attention.

In short, while hosting an NFL team can bring substantial economic benefits, it also involves considerable costs and risks. The true impact varies depending on the specific context, making it a complex and often controversial issue for the cities involved.

The Financial Dynamics of the Super Bowl

The Super Bowl is not just the pinnacle of American football; it is also a massive financial event that generates billions of dollars in revenue. The financial dynamics of the Super Bowl encompass a wide range of factors, from television broadcasting rights to sponsorships, advertisements, and the economic impact on the host city.

One of the largest sources of revenue for the Super Bowl is **television broadcasting rights**. The network that secures the rights to broadcast the game pays a substantial fee, often exceeding $100 million, for the privilege. This investment is justified by the Super Bowl's ability to draw one of the largest television audiences in the world, with over 100 million viewers in the United States alone. The massive viewership allows the network to charge top dollar for advertising slots, with a 30-second commercial costing upwards of $5 million. These advertisements are not only a major source of income but have also become a cultural phenomenon, with many viewers tuning in specifically to watch the commercials.

Sponsorship deals are another critical component of the Super Bowl's financial structure. Major brands pay significant amounts to be associated with the event, gaining exclusive rights to use the Super Bowl name and logo in their marketing. These sponsorships cover a wide range of categories, including beverages, automobiles, and telecommunications, with companies like Pepsi, Budweiser, and Verizon being long-time partners. The exclusivity of these deals allows sponsors to command a significant presence during the game, both in the stadium and through advertising.

The **economic impact on the host city** is another important financial aspect of the Super Bowl. Hosting the Super Bowl can inject hundreds of millions of dollars into the local economy, as fans, media, and corporate sponsors descend on the city. Hotels, restaurants, and local businesses see a surge in revenue, and the event often serves as a catalyst for infrastructure improvements. However, the costs of hosting, including security, transportation, and city services, can be substantial, leading to debates about the net benefit for the host city.

The financial dynamics of the Super Bowl are a testament to the event's immense popularity and cultural significance. It is a unique blend of sports, entertainment, and commerce that stands as one of the most lucrative and high-profile events in the world.

Sponsorship and Endorsement Deals

Sponsorship and endorsement deals are vital components of the NFL's business model, generating significant revenue for the league, teams, and individual players. These deals are a reflection of the NFL's powerful brand and its ability to reach a vast, engaged audience.

At the league level, the NFL secures **sponsorship deals** with major corporations, allowing them to associate their brands with the NFL's high-profile games and events. These partnerships cover a wide range of industries, including automotive, technology, and food and beverage. Companies like Nike, Pepsi, and Microsoft are among the league's most prominent sponsors, paying millions of dollars for the exclusive rights to market their products with the NFL's logos and trademarks. These deals are mutually beneficial, as they provide the NFL with substantial revenue while giving sponsors access to the league's massive fan base.

Teams also engage in **sponsorship deals** at a more localized level. These deals often involve stadium naming rights, local media partnerships, and agreements with regional businesses. For example, many NFL stadiums are named after corporate sponsors, such as **AT&T Stadium** in Dallas and **Gillette Stadium** in New England. These deals can be worth hundreds of millions of dollars and are crucial for teams looking to fund stadium renovations, player salaries, and other operational costs.

Endorsement deals play a significant role in the financial landscape for individual players. Top NFL players often sign lucrative endorsement contracts with companies looking to capitalize on their popularity and influence. These deals can involve everything from apparel and footwear to automobiles and consumer electronics. For instance, players like **Tom Brady** and **Patrick Mahomes** have secured multi-million-dollar endorsements with brands such as Under Armour and State Farm. These deals not only provide players with additional income but also enhance their personal brands, making them more marketable both during and after their playing careers.

The NFL's ability to attract and maintain high-value sponsorship and endorsement deals is a testament to its dominance in the sports industry. These deals are about building long-term partnerships that benefit the league, teams, players, and sponsors alike. The success of these relationships underscores the NFL's status as a powerful and influential force in the world of sports and business.

CHAPTER 16: THE LEGACY AND FUTURE OF AMERICAN FOOTBALL

The Hall of Fame and Honoring NFL Legends

The Pro Football Hall of Fame, located in Canton, Ohio, stands as the ultimate shrine to the legends of the NFL. It's a place where the greatest players, coaches, and contributors are honored for their extraordinary impact on the game. The Hall of Fame not only preserves the history of American football but also celebrates the achievements of those who have defined the sport.

Founded in 1963, the Hall of Fame serves as a testament to the evolution of the NFL and its role in American culture. The selection process for enshrinement is rigorous and highly selective. Each year, a panel of media members, football historians, and former players reviews the careers of eligible candidates, considering their accomplishments, influence, and contributions to the game. This process ensures that only the most deserving individuals are inducted, making it one of the highest honors in sports.

Induction into the Hall of Fame is a momentous occasion, often seen as the pinnacle of a football career. For players, it's an acknowledgment of their talent, dedication, and impact on the field. Legends like **Joe Montana, Jerry Rice**, and **Jim Brown** are immortalized here, their bronze busts serving as enduring symbols of their greatness. Coaches like **Bill Walsh** and **Vince Lombardi**, whose strategic innovations and leadership shaped the NFL, are also celebrated, alongside owners and contributors who have helped grow the league into the powerhouse it is today.

The Hall of Fame also is important in educating fans about the rich history of the NFL. Its exhibits showcase the evolution of the game, from its early days to the modern era, highlighting key moments, teams, and players that have left a lasting legacy. Interactive displays and memorabilia allow visitors to engage with the history of football in a meaningful way, deepening their appreciation for the sport.

The annual **Hall of Fame Game** and **Enshrinement Ceremony** are major events that draw fans, players, and media from across the country. The enshrinement ceremony, where new inductees deliver heartfelt speeches reflecting on their careers, is particularly emotional, offering a glimpse into the personal journeys of these football icons. It's a moment of reflection and celebration, not just for the inductees but for the entire football community.

The Hall of Fame is more than just a museum; it's a living tribute to the legends of the NFL. It honors those who have shaped the game, preserving their legacies for future generations. As the NFL continues to grow and evolve, the Hall of Fame remains a vital institution, ensuring that the contributions of its greatest figures are remembered and celebrated.

The Ongoing Debate Over Player Safety

The debate over player safety in the NFL has intensified in recent years, as growing awareness of the long-term effects of injuries, particularly concussions, has raised concerns about the physical toll of the game. The league has taken significant steps to address these issues, but the debate continues as to whether these measures are sufficient to protect players.

One of the central concerns in the player safety debate is the risk of **concussions and Chronic Traumatic Encephalopathy (CTE)**. Studies have shown that repeated head trauma, common in football, can lead to CTE, a degenerative brain disease associated with memory loss, depression, and cognitive decline. In response, the NFL has implemented stricter concussion protocols, introduced rule changes to reduce helmet-to-helmet hits, and invested in research to develop safer helmets.

However, despite these efforts, critics argue that the nature of football itself makes it inherently dangerous, and that the league's measures, while helpful, do not fully address the risks. Some suggest that more drastic changes, such as altering tackling techniques or even reducing the number of games in a season, are necessary to better protect players. Others point to the culture of toughness in football, which can discourage players from reporting injuries or taking time to recover.

The debate over player safety is not just about the present; it's also about the future of the sport. As the NFL faces increasing scrutiny from the public, players, and health professionals, it must continue to evolve its approach to player safety, balancing the intensity of the game with the well-being of its athletes.

The NFL's Role in Promoting Diversity and Inclusion

The NFL has taken a more active role in promoting diversity and inclusion, recognizing the importance of reflecting the diversity of its players and fan base in its leadership and organizational structures. The league's efforts have included initiatives aimed at increasing the representation of minorities and women in coaching, front-office positions, and beyond.

One of the most significant steps in this direction has been the implementation of the **Rooney Rule** in 2003, which requires NFL teams to interview at least one minority candidate for head coaching and senior football operation positions. While the rule has led to some progress, critics argue that its impact has been limited and that more needs to be done to ensure that minority candidates are not just considered but also hired.

In recent years, the NFL has expanded its efforts to promote diversity and inclusion through programs like the **Bill Walsh Diversity Coaching Fellowship**, which provides opportunities for minority coaches to gain experience and exposure. The league has also focused on increasing the number of women in leadership roles, both within the NFL and across its teams, acknowledging that diverse perspectives lead to stronger, more innovative organizations.

Beyond the league office, the NFL has supported player-led initiatives that address social justice issues, including the fight against racial inequality. The league's **Inspire Change** program, for example, funds organizations working in areas such as education, economic advancement, and criminal justice reform.

The NFL's role in promoting diversity and inclusion is an ongoing effort. While progress has been made, the league continues to face challenges in achieving true equity. As the NFL looks to the future, its commitment to diversity and inclusion will be crucial in ensuring that the sport remains relevant and respected in an increasingly diverse society.

The Evolution of NFL Coaching and Strategy

The evolution of NFL coaching and strategy has been marked by constant innovation, adaptation, and a deep understanding of the game's changing dynamics. From the early days of simple formations and ground-and-pound football to today's complex, high-flying offenses and versatile defenses, the role of the coach has evolved into that of a strategist, leader, and innovator.

In the early years of the NFL, coaching was straightforward, with a strong emphasis on the running game. The most successful teams relied on powerful offensive lines and dominant running backs. Coaches like **George Halas** and **Curly Lambeau** were pioneers in developing basic offensive and defensive schemes, but the game was largely about physical dominance rather than strategic complexity.

The first major shift in coaching strategy came with the advent of the **T-formation** in the 1940s, popularized by **George Halas** and his assistant, **Clark Shaughnessy**. The T-formation revolutionized the game by introducing the concept of a quarterback taking snaps directly under center, which allowed for more effective passing and running plays. This innovation led to the rise of the passing game and changed the way offenses were designed, making the quarterback a central figure in the game's strategy.

The 1960s and 1970s saw another significant evolution with the introduction of the **West Coast Offense**, developed by **Bill Walsh**. The West Coast Offense emphasized short, quick passes to control the ball and move methodically down the field. It relied on timing, precision, and the ability to gain yards after the catch. Walsh's approach transformed the NFL, leading to the dominance of the **San Francisco 49ers** in the 1980s and influencing countless other coaches and teams.

On the defensive side, the evolution of coaching strategy has been equally transformative. The 1980s and 1990s brought the rise of complex defensive schemes like the **46 defense** created by **Buddy Ryan** and the **zone blitz** popularized by **Dick LeBeau**. These strategies emphasized aggressive, unpredictable attacks on the quarterback while disguising coverages, making it difficult for offenses to read the defense. The **46 defense** was instrumental in the Chicago Bears' dominance during their 1985 Super Bowl-winning season, while the zone blitz became a staple for defenses like the Pittsburgh Steelers.

The 2000s and 2010s saw further evolution in NFL coaching and strategy, driven by advances in technology and analytics. Coaches like **Bill Belichick** of the New England Patriots became known for their meticulous game planning and adaptability. Belichick's approach to situational football, where decisions are made based on specific game scenarios, set a new standard for coaching in the NFL. His use of versatile players who can excel in multiple roles also became a blueprint for modern coaching.

The spread offense, which originated in college football, made its way to the NFL in the 2010s, emphasizing wide formations, quick passes, and the use of mobile quarterbacks. This strategy put pressure on defenses by stretching them horizontally and exploiting mismatches in space. Coaches like **Andy Reid** and **Sean McVay** have been at the forefront of this trend, using the spread offense to create high-powered, dynamic attacks that are difficult to defend.

In addition to these offensive and defensive innovations, the use of **data analytics** has revolutionized NFL coaching strategy. Teams now use advanced statistical models to inform play-calling, player evaluation, and game management decisions. Analytics have become an essential tool for modern coaches, helping them to identify tendencies, optimize strategies, and gain a competitive edge.

The evolution of NFL coaching and strategy is a testament to the game's complexity and the continual quest for innovation. As the NFL moves forward, coaches will continue to adapt and innovate, pushing the boundaries of what is possible on the football field. The strategies that define the game today will evolve as new ideas, technologies, and player talents emerge, ensuring that the NFL remains a dynamic and ever-changing sport.

The Future of American Football: Challenges and Opportunities

The future of American football is marked by both significant challenges and exciting opportunities as the sport continues to evolve in the 21st century. One of the most pressing challenges is **player safety**, particularly regarding concussions and the long-term effects of repeated head trauma. As medical research continues to shed light on the dangers of CTE, the NFL must balance maintaining the physical intensity of the game with implementing measures to protect players. Innovations in helmet technology, rule changes, and education on safer tackling techniques are crucial steps in addressing these concerns.

Another challenge is the **shifting landscape of media consumption**. As younger audiences increasingly favor streaming and on-demand content over traditional television, the NFL must adapt its broadcasting and digital strategies to meet these changing preferences. The league's partnerships with streaming platforms and its own NFL Game Pass service are steps in the right direction, but continuing to innovate in this area will be essential to maintaining and growing its audience.

On the opportunity side, the NFL's **global expansion** presents a significant growth avenue. The success of international games in London and Mexico City demonstrates the sport's appeal beyond the United States. Expanding these efforts, possibly by establishing a permanent team abroad, could open new markets and further solidify American football as a global sport.

Additionally, the increasing use of **technology and data analytics** in player development, game strategy, and fan engagement offers new ways to enhance the sport. From wearable technology that monitors player health to advanced analytics that inform coaching decisions, these innovations will play a key role in the future of football.

So while American football faces challenges, it also has numerous opportunities to innovate and grow. The sport's ability to adapt to these changes will determine its continued success in the years to come.

CHAPTER 17: AMERICAN FOOTBALL TIMELINES

Timeline of Major Events in Football's Evolution

This timeline captures the major milestones in American football from the 1800s through the 2020s, highlighting the sport's evolution into a global phenomenon and addressing the challenges and opportunities that have shaped the modern NFL.

1800s

- **1869:** The first intercollegiate football game is played between Rutgers and Princeton on November 6, marking the beginning of organized college football. The game resembled a mix of soccer and rugby, with a round ball and 25 players on each side.
- **1876:** The Intercollegiate Football Association (IFA) is formed by representatives from Harvard, Yale, Princeton, and Columbia. The IFA establishes the first standard rules for American football, which begin to diverge from rugby.
- **1880: Walter Camp**, often referred to as the "Father of American Football," introduces key rule changes, including the line of scrimmage, the snap from center to quarterback, and reducing the number of players on each team from 15 to 11. These changes significantly differentiate American football from rugby.
- **1882:** The concept of downs is introduced by Walter Camp, requiring a team to advance the ball a certain distance (initially five yards in three downs) to retain possession. This rule lays the foundation for the modern game's structure.

1900s-1920s

- **1905:** Amid growing concerns about the brutality of the sport, President **Theodore Roosevelt** intervenes, urging colleges to reform football rules to make the game safer. This leads to the establishment of the **National Collegiate Athletic Association (NCAA)** and significant rule changes, including the legalization of the forward pass in 1906.
- **1920:** The **American Professional Football Association (APFA)** is formed on September 17 in Canton, Ohio. This league later becomes the National Football League (NFL) in 1922, marking the official birth of professional football in the United States.
- **1925: Red Grange**, a star college football player, signs with the Chicago Bears, bringing legitimacy and widespread attention to professional football. His barnstorming tours help popularize the NFL.

- **1932:** The NFL holds its first official championship game, played indoors at Chicago Stadium due to poor weather. The success of this game leads to the establishment of an annual NFL Championship Game, setting the stage for the eventual creation of the Super Bowl.

1930s-1940s

- **1936:** The NFL holds its first draft, introducing a system where teams select players in reverse order of their performance from the previous season. This draft aims to maintain competitive balance across the league.
- **1941:** The NFL adopts a new playoff format, introducing divisional play and a championship game between division winners, further solidifying the league's structure.
- **1946:** The **All-America Football Conference (AAFC)** is founded, becoming a significant rival to the NFL. The AAFC's competition forces the NFL to improve its operations and expand to new markets.
- **1949:** The NFL and AAFC merge, with three AAFC teams (the Cleveland Browns, San Francisco 49ers, and Baltimore Colts) joining the NFL. This merger strengthens the NFL and expands its reach.

1950s

- **1950:** The NFL integrates, with the Los Angeles Rams and the Washington Redskins becoming the last teams to sign African American players. This marks a significant step toward racial equality in the league.
- **1958:** The NFL Championship Game between the Baltimore Colts and New York Giants, often called "The Greatest Game Ever Played," is held. The game goes into sudden-death overtime, and its thrilling conclusion captivates a national television audience, helping to propel the NFL into mainstream popularity.
- **1959:** **Lamar Hunt** founds the American Football League (AFL) after being denied an NFL expansion franchise. The AFL introduces new ideas and innovations, leading to a decade of competition with the NFL.

1960s

- **1960:** The **American Football League (AFL)** officially begins play with eight teams. The AFL introduces innovations such as the two-point conversion and a more pass-oriented offensive style, challenging the NFL's dominance.
- **1963:** The Pro Football Hall of Fame opens in Canton, Ohio, honoring the greatest figures in the history of the sport and preserving its legacy.
- **1966:** The NFL and AFL announce a merger agreement, set to take effect in 1970. As part of the agreement, the two leagues agree to hold an annual championship game, which becomes known as the Super Bowl.

- **1967:** The first Super Bowl, officially called the AFL-NFL World Championship Game, is held on January 15. The NFL's Green Bay Packers defeat the AFL's Kansas City Chiefs. The game establishes the Super Bowl as the premier event in American sports.
- **1968:** The **"Heidi Game"** occurs on November 17, when NBC cuts away from the New York Jets-Oakland Raiders game to air the movie "Heidi," missing the Raiders' dramatic comeback. The incident leads to changes in how networks handle live sports broadcasts, ensuring that games are shown in their entirety.

1970s

- **1970:** The NFL-AFL merger is completed, creating a unified league with two conferences, the NFC and AFC. The first post-merger Super Bowl, Super Bowl V, is played in January 1971, with the Baltimore Colts defeating the Dallas Cowboys.
- **1972:** The Miami Dolphins complete the only perfect season in NFL history, finishing 17-0 and winning Super Bowl VII. This achievement remains unmatched and solidifies the Dolphins' place in football lore.
- **1974:** The NFL introduces several key rule changes, including the **"Mel Blount Rule,"** which limits defensive contact with receivers, and the introduction of sudden-death overtime in regular-season games. These changes are designed to increase scoring and improve the flow of the game.
- **1978:** The NFL further liberalizes the passing game by allowing offensive linemen to extend their arms when blocking and increasing the enforcement of the illegal contact rule against defenders. These changes contribute to the rise of high-powered passing offenses in the league.

1980s

- **1982:** A players' strike reduces the regular season to nine games, but the NFL introduces an expanded playoff format called the "Super Bowl Tournament," which includes 16 teams. This marks a significant moment in the league's labor relations history.
- **1985:** The Chicago Bears dominate the NFL with a suffocating defense, known as the **"46 defense,"** and a charismatic coach in Mike Ditka. The Bears win Super Bowl XX and become one of the most iconic teams in NFL history.
- **1986:** The NFL introduces **instant replay** as an officiating tool, allowing referees to review certain plays using video footage. This system is the precursor to the modern instant replay rules that help ensure the accuracy of calls on the field.
- **1989:** **Jerry Jones** purchases the Dallas Cowboys and hires **Jimmy Johnson** as head coach. This partnership leads to the Cowboys' resurgence in the early 1990s, culminating in three Super Bowl victories.

1990s

- **1993:** The NFL and NFL Players Association (NFLPA) agree to a new collective bargaining agreement that introduces **free agency**, allowing players greater freedom to sign with new teams. This change fundamentally alters team-building strategies across the league.
- **1994:** The NFL introduces the **salary cap**, a system designed to promote competitive balance by limiting the total amount teams can spend on player salaries. The salary cap remains a key component of the NFL's financial structure.
- **1999:** The St. Louis Rams, led by quarterback **Kurt Warner** and known as the **"Greatest Show on Turf,"** win Super Bowl XXXIV, showcasing a high-octane offense that sets numerous records and influences future offensive strategies.
- **1999:** The Cleveland Browns return to the NFL as an expansion team after the original Browns franchise relocated to Baltimore and became the Ravens in 1996. The new Browns are granted the history and records of the original franchise.

2000s

- **2001: Tom Brady** leads the New England Patriots to victory in Super Bowl XXXVI, beginning a dynasty that would see the Patriots win six Super Bowls over two decades under head coach **Bill Belichick**.
- **2007:** The NFL introduces the **International Series**, with the first regular-season game played outside North America in London, England. The series expands the NFL's global reach and becomes a regular part of the league's schedule.
- **2007:** The New England Patriots complete an undefeated regular season (16-0) but lose to the New York Giants in Super Bowl XLII, one of the biggest upsets in NFL history.
- **2011:** A lockout threatens the 2011 season, but the NFL and NFLPA reach a new collective bargaining agreement, preserving labor peace and introducing new safety measures, revenue-sharing adjustments, and an expanded regular-season schedule.

2010s

- **2012:** The NFL enforces new rules to address player safety, particularly concerning concussions and head injuries. The league's focus on health and safety leads to significant rule changes, including stricter enforcement of helmet-to-helmet hits and the expansion of concussion protocols.
- **2016: Colin Kaepernick** sparks a national conversation about racial inequality and police brutality by kneeling during the national anthem. His protest and the subsequent player activism lead to widespread discussions about the NFL's role in social justice issues.

- **2017:** The NFL reaches a new peak in global popularity, with the Super Bowl LI between the New England Patriots and the Atlanta Falcons becoming one of the most-watched events in television history. The game is also notable for the Patriots' historic comeback from a 28-3 deficit.
- **2018:** The NFL introduces a new rule making it illegal for players to lower their heads to initiate contact with their helmets. This rule is part of the league's ongoing efforts to reduce head injuries and promote player safety.

2020s

- **2020:** The NFL adapts to the COVID-19 pandemic by implementing strict health protocols, holding games without fans or with limited attendance, and introducing flexible scheduling to accommodate postponements. The league successfully completes the season, culminating in Super Bowl LV.
- **2021:** The NFL expands the regular season to 17 games, the first major schedule change since the 1978 expansion to 16 games. This move is part of a broader effort to increase revenue and maintain the league's growth.
- **2022:** The NFL continues its focus on diversity and inclusion by enhancing the **Rooney Rule** and increasing efforts to promote minority hiring in coaching and executive positions. The league also faces ongoing challenges related to player safety, social justice, and global expansion.

Timeline of Strategic Evolutions in Football

This timeline outlines the key strategic evolutions in American football from its inception in the 1800s through the 1950s. These developments set the stage for the modern game, introducing concepts and formations that would build off each other in the years and decades to come.

1800s

- **1869:** The first intercollegiate football game between Rutgers and Princeton is played, marking the beginning of organized American football. The game closely resembles a blend of soccer and rugby, with limited strategy beyond basic formations and scrums.
- **1876:** The Intercollegiate Football Association (IFA) standardizes rules that begin to distinguish American football from rugby. The emphasis is still on brute strength and simple formations, but the foundations of a more structured game start to emerge.
- **1880: Walter Camp**, known as the "Father of American Football," introduces the **line of scrimmage** and the **snap** from center to quarterback, which fundamentally change the game's strategy. These innovations allow for more organized plays and set the stage for the development of offensive and defensive strategies.

- **1882:** Walter Camp further refines the game by introducing the concept of **downs**, requiring teams to advance the ball five yards in three plays to retain possession. This rule forces teams to think more strategically about each play, balancing the risk and reward of different types of plays.

1900s-1920s

- **1906:** The forward pass is legalized in response to concerns about the safety of the game. Initially met with resistance, the forward pass begins to open up new strategic possibilities, although it will take decades before it becomes a central part of the game.
- **1913:** Notre Dame's upset victory over Army, led by coach **Jesse Harper** and quarterback **Knute Rockne**, showcases the effectiveness of the forward pass as a strategic weapon. This game is a turning point, demonstrating that passing can be more than just a trick play.
- **1920s:** The **single-wing formation**, developed by **Glenn "Pop" Warner**, becomes one of the most popular and influential offensive schemes. It emphasizes misdirection, power running, and occasional passing, making it a versatile and effective strategy for the era.
- **1920s:** The **formation of the NFL** in 1920 and its early years see a continuation of college football strategies, with most professional teams still relying heavily on running plays and simple formations. However, coaches begin to experiment with different strategies to gain a competitive edge.

1930s-1940s

- **1933:** The NFL legalizes **forward passing from anywhere behind the line of scrimmage** (previously restricted to certain areas), leading to a gradual increase in the use of passing as a strategic tool. This rule change marks the beginning of the transition to a more balanced offensive strategy.
- **1936:** The **T-formation** re-emerges as a dominant offensive strategy, popularized by **Clark Shaughnessy** and **George Halas** with the Chicago Bears. The T-formation allows for a more sophisticated passing game and introduces the concept of the quarterback as a field general, making decisions based on the defense's alignment.
- **1940:** The Chicago Bears, using the T-formation, defeat the Washington Redskins 73-0 in the NFL Championship Game, demonstrating the formation's strategic superiority. This victory signals a shift in the NFL, as more teams begin to adopt the T-formation.
- **1943:** The **"man-in-motion"** rule is introduced, allowing one offensive player to move laterally or backward before the snap. This adds a new dimension to offensive strategy, enabling teams to create misdirection and disguise their intentions more effectively.

- **1947:** The NFL introduces **two-platoon football**, allowing separate units for offense and defense. This change leads to greater specialization and more complex strategies on both sides of the ball, as players focus exclusively on their specific roles.

1950s

- **1950:** The **Cleveland Browns**, led by coach **Paul Brown**, dominate the NFL using innovative strategies such as **precision passing**, the use of **playbooks** and **film study**, and the introduction of the **draw play**. Brown's approach to coaching and game preparation lays the groundwork for modern football strategy.
- **1956: Tom Landry** introduces the **4-3 defense** as the defensive coordinator for the New York Giants. The 4-3 defense, which uses four linemen and three linebackers, becomes one of the most widely adopted defensive strategies in football, valued for its flexibility against both the run and the pass.
- **1958:** The NFL Championship Game between the Baltimore Colts and New York Giants, often called "The Greatest Game Ever Played," showcases the evolution of football strategy, with teams employing more sophisticated passing offenses and defenses. The game goes into sudden-death overtime and is seen by many as a turning point in the popularity and strategic complexity of the NFL.

1960s

- **1960:** The American Football League (AFL) introduces a more **wide-open offensive style**, emphasizing the passing game more than the NFL. The AFL's approach, which includes deep passing and spread formations, challenges traditional NFL strategies and eventually influences the merged league.
- **1961: Vince Lombardi's** Green Bay Packers popularize the **power sweep**, a running play that becomes synonymous with Lombardi's teams. The play, which features guards pulling to lead the running back around the edge, emphasizes disciplined blocking and execution, showcasing the importance of precision in offensive strategy.
- **1963:** The **West Coast Offense**, initially developed by **Sid Gillman** and later perfected by **Bill Walsh**, begins to take shape. This offense emphasizes short, timing-based passes that function as extensions of the running game, creating a more efficient and controlled offensive attack.
- **1966:** The NFL and AFL agree to merge, leading to the blending of different strategic approaches. The AFL's passing innovations begin to influence NFL teams, leading to a more dynamic and balanced offensive strategy across the league.
- **1969: Tom Landry** of the Dallas Cowboys refines the **Flex Defense**, a variation of the 4-3 alignment. The Flex Defense is designed to counter the

run-heavy offenses of the time by allowing the defensive line to adjust based on the offense's movements, demonstrating the increasing complexity of defensive strategy.

1970s

- **1970:** The **NFL-AFL merger** is completed, creating a unified league with two conferences. The merger leads to the standardization of strategies and playbooks across the league, with teams incorporating elements from both leagues' approaches.
- **1972: Don Shula's** Miami Dolphins complete the NFL's only perfect season using a **balanced offensive attack** and a dominant defense. Shula's emphasis on adaptability and game-specific strategies becomes a model for future coaches.
- **1974:** The NFL introduces **sudden-death overtime** for regular-season games, adding a new strategic element to end-game scenarios. Coaches must now account for the possibility of overtime when making decisions late in the game.
- **1978:** The NFL makes significant rule changes to promote the passing game, including allowing **offensive linemen to extend their arms in pass protection** and limiting contact between defensive backs and receivers. These changes lead to a more explosive and wide-open style of play, setting the stage for the rise of the modern passing game.
- **1979:** The **Pittsburgh Steelers** win their fourth Super Bowl using a combination of **Terry Bradshaw's** vertical passing game and the **Steel Curtain defense**. The Steelers' success highlights the importance of balance between offense and defense in strategic planning.

1980s

- **1980:** The **West Coast Offense** reaches its full potential under **Bill Walsh** and the San Francisco 49ers. This offense emphasizes quick, short passes and precise timing, allowing quarterbacks like **Joe Montana** to efficiently move the ball downfield. The West Coast Offense becomes one of the most influential strategies in NFL history.
- **1985: Buddy Ryan** introduces the **46 defense** with the Chicago Bears, a hyper-aggressive scheme that uses eight men near the line of scrimmage to overwhelm the offense. The 46 defense leads the Bears to a Super Bowl victory and becomes a model for aggressive defensive play.
- **1986:** The **zone blitz** is developed by **Dick LeBeau**, defensive coordinator for the Cincinnati Bengals. The zone blitz combines the unpredictability of blitzing with zone coverage, allowing defenses to pressure the quarterback while still covering receivers. This strategy becomes a staple in defensive playbooks across the league.
- **1988:** The **no-huddle offense** is popularized by the **Cincinnati Bengals** under head coach **Sam Wyche** and offensive coordinator **Bruce Coslet**.

This up-tempo strategy forces defenses to remain on the field without substitutions, creating mismatches and tiring out opponents. The no-huddle offense is later perfected by **Jim Kelly's** Buffalo Bills in the 1990s.

1990s

- **1990:** The **zone running scheme** gains prominence under **Mike Shanahan** and the Denver Broncos. This strategy emphasizes offensive linemen blocking in unison to create cutback lanes for the running back. The zone running scheme, paired with a strong passing game, leads to two Super Bowl titles for the Broncos in the late 1990s.
- **1993:** The NFL introduces **free agency**, leading to more player movement and forcing teams to adapt their strategies based on roster turnover. Coaches and general managers must now prioritize flexibility in both offensive and defensive schemes to accommodate new personnel.
- **1999:** The **St. Louis Rams**, led by offensive coordinator **Mike Martz**, introduce the **Greatest Show on Turf** offense. This high-powered passing attack, featuring quarterback **Kurt Warner** and wide receiver **Isaac Bruce**, emphasizes deep passes and spread formations, revolutionizing the modern passing game.

2000s

- **2001: Bill Belichick** and the New England Patriots introduce a **flexible, game-specific defensive approach** that emphasizes adaptability. Belichick's use of versatile players and complex coverages, combined with situational football, helps the Patriots win six Super Bowls over two decades.
- **2004:** The **Wildcat formation** is revived by the Miami Dolphins, adding an element of surprise and unpredictability to offensive strategy. This direct-snap formation to a running back briefly becomes a popular trend, demonstrating the ongoing evolution of offensive creativity.
- **2007:** The **New England Patriots** perfect the **spread offense**, using a combination of short, quick passes and deep threats like **Randy Moss**. This offense sets numerous records and changes how teams approach the passing game, emphasizing the importance of spreading the field and creating mismatches.
- **2009:** The **New Orleans Saints**, led by head coach **Sean Payton**, win the Super Bowl using an aggressive offensive strategy and creative play-calling, including the famous **onside kick** to start the second half of Super Bowl XLIV. Payton's approach highlights the importance of risk-taking and innovation in modern coaching.

2010s

- **2012:** The **read-option offense** becomes a significant trend in the NFL, popularized by quarterbacks like **Cam Newton** and **Robert Griffin III**. This strategy, which allows the quarterback to read the defense and decide whether to hand off, pass, or run, adds a new dimension to offensive playbooks.
- **2013:** The **Seattle Seahawks** dominate with the **Legion of Boom** defense, using a combination of press coverage, a strong pass rush, and physical play to win Super Bowl XLVIII. The Seahawks' success emphasizes the continued importance of defense, even in an increasingly pass-happy league.
- **2017:** **RPOs (Run-Pass Options)** gain popularity, giving quarterbacks the ability to decide between running or passing based on the defense's reaction. This strategy becomes a staple in modern offenses, allowing for greater flexibility and adaptability on the field.
- **2018: Patrick Mahomes** and the Kansas City Chiefs, under head coach **Andy Reid**, revolutionize offensive strategy with a combination of **deep passing, motion-based plays, and innovative formations**. The Chiefs' explosive offense, paired with Mahomes' unique arm talent, sets new standards for offensive creativity in the NFL.

2020s

- **2020:** The **spread offense** continues to dominate the league, with teams like the Kansas City Chiefs and Buffalo Bills using wide formations and versatile playmakers to stretch defenses horizontally and vertically. This evolution builds on trends from the 2000s and 2010s, with even more emphasis on speed and space.
- **2020:** The NFL adapts to the COVID-19 pandemic by introducing **virtual coaching and player meetings**, showing how technology can play a role in strategic planning and game preparation. Teams that embrace these new methods find success in a challenging environment.
- **2021:** The NFL expands the regular season to 17 games, forcing teams to adjust their strategies for managing player health and depth over a longer season. Coaches must now balance maintaining peak performance with the physical demands of an extended schedule.
- **2022-24:** The continued evolution of **positionless football** sees players like **Deebo Samuel** and **Christian McCaffery** of the San Francisco 49ers playing multiple roles, such as wide receiver and running back. This trend towards versatility and unpredictability challenges traditional positional definitions and adds complexity to both offensive and defensive strategies.

This timeline outlines the major strategic evolutions in American football from the 1800s through the 2020s, showcasing the innovations and adjustments that have shaped the modern game. These strategies continue to influence how teams approach both offense and defense, ensuring that football remains dynamic and ever-changing.

AFTERWORD

Well, folks, we've reached the final whistle of our journey through the history of American football and the NFL.

We started with a bunch of college kids running around with an oddly-shaped ball in a game that looked much closer to soccer, and now we're in an era of multi-billion dollar franchises, global superstars, and a game that's watched by millions around the world. It's pretty amazing when you think about it.

Throughout this book, we've seen how football has grown and changed. We've met the pioneers who shaped the game, celebrated the iconic moments that define its history, and explored the challenges it's faced along the way. From the muddy fields of the early days to the high-tech stadiums of today, we've covered lots of ground.

But as I write this, and as you read it, the game is still evolving. New stars are emerging, new strategies are being developed, and new chapters in the NFL's history are being written every season. That's part of what makes being a football fan so exciting – you never know what's going to happen next.

I hope this book has given you a deeper appreciation for the game. Maybe you've gained some new insights into why certain rules exist, or you've found a new appreciation for the players of yesteryear. Perhaps you've even found some parallels between the challenges of the past and the issues facing the sport today.

More than anything, I hope this book has reminded you of why you love football. Whether it's the thrill of a last-minute touchdown, the satisfaction of seeing a perfectly executed play, or just the joy of sharing a game day with friends and family – football has a special way of bringing people together and creating unforgettable moments.

So, what's next for football? Well, that's the exciting part – we don't know! Will we see more international games? New technologies changing how we watch and play? Maybe even new teams or leagues? Will we ever get an international team? Whatever happens, you can bet it'll be exciting.

As we close this book, remember that you're now part of this ongoing story. Every time you watch a game, cheer for your team, or toss a football around in the backyard, you're adding your own little chapter to the grand history of American football.

Printed in Great Britain
by Amazon

48349738R00076